BETRAYED BY THE BENCH

BETRAYED BY THE BENCH

How Judge-made Law Has Transformed America's Constitution, Courts and Culture

By

John A. Stormer

LIBERTY BELL PRESS

Florissant, Missouri

ALSO BY JOHN STORMER

None Dare Call It Treason
The Anatomy of a Smear
The Death of a Nation
Growing Up God's Way
None Dare Call It Treason—25 YEARS LATER
None Dare Call It Education

BETRAYED BY THE BENCH

Hardcover Library Edition Copyright - 2005 by John A. Stormer
ISBN 978-0-914053-17-5

LIBERTY BELL PRESS

Post Office Box 32
Florissant MO 63032

Library of Congress Cataloging-in-Publication Data

John A. Stormer

Betrayed by the Bench

Includes Index
1. Supreme Court 2. Judge-made Law 3. Declaration of Independence
4. Constitution 5. Abortion

Title

Paper Cover Edition - September 2007
PRINTED IN THE UNITED STATES OF AMERICA
Paper Cover Edition - ISBN 978-0-914053-18-3

ABOUT THE AUTHOR

In 1962, John Stormer left a successful career as editor and general manager of a leading electrical magazine to write. His first book, *None Dare Call It Treason,* was a runaway best-seller in 1964. It was widely distributed by those supporting the Presidential campaign of Senator Barry Goldwater. Many prominent people credit reading *None Dare Call It Treason* with inspiring them to enter public life, the ministry, etc.

His five books have sold over eleven million copies.

As a best selling author, pastor and Christian school superintendent John Stormer has encouraged many to fulfill their responsibilities to the Lord, their families and America.

Since 1977 John Stormer has conducted weekly Bible studies in the Missouri Capitol in Jefferson City for legislators.

He publishes *Understanding the Times,* a periodic newsletter analyzing significant news developments in foreign policy, politics, education, religion and economics. He speaks regularly in Bible conferences and *Understanding the Times* seminars.

A native of Altoona, Pennsylvania, he attended the Pennsylvania State University and graduated from California San Jose State University after Korean War service as an Air Force historian and editor. He is listed in *Who's Who In America* and is a member of the American Legion, Rotary International and the Council for National Policy. He has honorary degrees from Manahath School of Theology (1965) and Shelton College (1976). He and his wife, Elizabeth, are 50 years residents of Florissant, Missouri, a St. Louis suburb. Their daughter, Holly, is married and the mother of their four grandchildren.

DEDICATION

Forty years ago, my first book was dedicated to my daughter Holly with the hope that her future might be as bright as mine was at age five.

The next to last page of that book quoted

II Chronicles 7:14 where God says:

If my people, which are called by my name, shall humble themselves and pray and seek my face, and turn from their wicked ways: then will I hear from heaven, and will forgive their sin, and will heal their land.

America still has not been healed. The peril America faces may be greater today than it was 40 years ago. Today, it is the future of my grandchildren about whom I am concerned.

CONTENTS

The vision and intent of America's Founding Fathers, as expressed in the Declaration of Independence and the Constitution, have been betrayed. Judges—from the lowest courts to those who sit on the bench of the Supreme Court no longer uphold the standards of morality, decency and freedom on which America grew great.
America must return to her roots, and soon.

WHAT HAPPENS WHEN JUDGES VIOLATE THE OATH OF OFFICE?

OATH: A solemn affirmation or declaration, made with an appeal to God for the truth of what is affirmed. The appeal to God in an oath, implies that the person requests God's vengeance and renounces God's favor if the declaration is false. If the declaration is a promise, the person invokes the vengeance of God if he should fail to fulfill it.
BETRAY: To violate by fraud, or unfaithfulness, as to betray a trust.
Noah Webster — 1828 Dictionary

THE UNITED STATES WAS ESTABLISHED on a foundation which was different from that of any nation in history. The second paragraph of the *Declaration of Independence* sets America apart. It says:

> *We hold these truths to be self-evident, that all men are created equal, <u>that they are endowed by their Creator with certain un-alienable rights,</u> that among these are Life, Liberty and the pursuit of Happiness.—That to secure these rights, Governments are instituted among Men, deriving their just powers from the consent of the governed.*

Every American's rights come from God—not from a king, not from the government nor even from the Constitution. Every judge takes an oath to uphold the U.S. Constitution. The Declaration says the Constitution was to be written to make God-given rights secure. That being so...

> *...how can judges or courts find "rights" to abort babies in the Constitution—violating what the Declaration of Independence says is the baby's God-given right to life?*

That question should be being asked by every citizen, by the media, by schools and in the Courts. A related question is: How can judges find in the Constitution written to make God-given rights secure, "rights" for people to engage in sodomy, distribute pornography or have same sex marriages? Would God give "rights" to do what He calls sin?

The Supreme Court has also ruled that praying or reading the Bible in school and the posting of the Ten Commandments are all unconstitutional. How can judges make such decisions? The *Declaration of Independence* is the foundation from which the U.S. Constitution should be interpreted and applied. Chapter II of this book shows why.

Chief Justice Charles Evans Hughes told why God-given rights are no longer "secure." In the 1920s Hughes said:

> *We are under a constitution, but the constitution is what we say it is.*[1]

The Supreme Court's attacks on the public acknowledgement of God and its legalization of abortion and sodomy are just the tip of an iceberg. Other vital constitutional principles have been ignored or replaced by activist judicial "interpretations" or edicts.

Roscoe Pound was dean of the Harvard Law School from 1916 to 1936. During his twenty year term at Harvard he oversaw the training of thousands of influential attorneys and judges. In a 1924 book he spelled out the philosophy in which future lawyers were trained. He wrote:

> *...the state is the unchallengeable authority behind legal precepts. The state takes the place of Jehovah handing down the tables of the law to Moses.*[2]

Pound's goal was using judge-made law to make government the supreme ultimate authority. It was to be done by removing God from His historical place as the giver of rights. How judges have done it is examined in Chapter VI.

Thomas Jefferson pointed to the danger in an 1819 letter when he wrote:

> *The Constitution is a mere thing of wax in the hands of the judiciary, which they may twist and shape into any form they please.*[3]

Over a fifty year period, the U.S. Supreme Court has been twisting and reshaping the Constitution. In the process, the right of individual States and their people to govern themselves has been transferred from the States to Washington and its federal courts.

The authority of individual States to control education and schools, the conduct of elections, highways, supervision of the criminal justice system, anti-pornography laws, financing and control of welfare programs, etc. has been transferred from the States to Washington and its federal courts. These are areas which the sovereign States had carefully reserved for themselves by adopting the Ninth and Tenth Amendments to the Constitution. Those amendments were designed, written and adopted to create a "wall of separation" between the States and the new federal government the States were creating. Those two amendments carefully reserved for the States and people all authority which the States had not given specifically to the federal government.

Thomas Jefferson feared that federal courts would tear down that "wall of separation." In an 1821 letter, Jefferson wrote...

> ...*the germ of the dissolution of our Federal government is in the constitution of the Federal judiciary—an irresponsible body...advancing its noiseless step like a thief over the field of jurisdiction until all shall be usurped from the States and the government shall be consolidated into one. To this I am opposed.*[4]

In an 1823 letter to Judge William Johnson, Jefferson explained why the founders built that constitutional "wall of separation" between the States and the new federal government. He said that they created the "wall" because they believed that...

> ...*the States can best govern our home concerns, and the general [federal] government our foreign ones.*[5]

That constitutional "wall of separation" has been breached repeatedly. It has been done not by constitutional amendments but by Supreme Court decisions. The nine-member U.S. Supreme Court has been overturning what the States created. The Court has made itself, in practice, an on-going Constitutional Convention. Again and again in recent years, often by 5-4 votes, the U.S. Supreme Court has, in effect, amended the Constitution by its decisions.

In a 2004 TV special, Judge Robert Bork charged:

> *The Constitution is being rewritten by judges.*[6]

Concerns really started surfacing in the early 1960s when the Supreme Court outlawed State laws which had always allowed prayer and Bible reading in their public schools.[7] The concern and outrage of some turned to dismay in 1973. That's when the Court in its *Roe v. Wade* decision[8] took the next step. *Roe v. Wade* struck down long standing State laws banning abortion. Since then...

> *...more babies die every day in the wombs of their mothers than were killed in the 9/11 attacks. Over 3,000 died that awful day in the terrorist attacks on the Twin Towers and the Pentagon. That many babies now die every day in abortion "clinics."*

The *Roe v. Wade* decision isn't the only federal court infringement on traditional state jurisdictions. In its 2003 *Lawrence v. Texas* decision the Court ruled that laws against sodomy in Texas and other States were unconstitutional.[9] For the first time in over 200 years the Supreme Court found that the Constitution provides...

> *...a right to engage in sodomy, a health threatening, AIDs producing perversion which God calls "sin."*

That same year the Massachusetts Supreme Court "discovered" that its 200-year old State constitution contained a "right" for same sex couples to marry.[10]

Earlier Supreme Court rulings had said that public acknowledgement of God is unconstitutional. Since then, lower courts have even put restrictions on the rights of little children to acknowledge God. In one such case in 2003...

> *...the 3rd Circuit Federal Court of Appeals ruled that an Egg Harbor, New Jersey school district was constitutionally correct when it stopped a kindergarten student, David Walz, from distributing pencils which said, "Jesus Loves Little Children" to classmates at a holiday party at school.*[11]

Banning the posting of the Ten Commandments in the schools was the landmark ruling. It came in 1980. (Chapter IX has a detailed examination of the Supreme Court's anti-God, anti-morality decisions.) A closing paragraph from the Supreme Court's Ten Commandments decision shows the anti-God bias. The Court's *Stone v. Graham* ruling says:

> *If the posted copies of the Ten Commandments are to have any effect at all, it will be to induce the school children to read, meditate upon, and perhaps venerate and obey, the Command-*

ments....not a permissible state objective under the Establishment Clause.[12]

How would today's Supreme Court respond to the words of James Madison, the fourth president of the United States? Madison is regarded as the principal author of the U.S. Constitution *and* the First Amendment. He said:

> *We have staked the whole future of American civilization not upon the power of government, far from it. We have staked the future of our political institutions upon the capacity of mankind for self-government; upon the capacity of each and all of us to govern ourselves, to control ourselves, to sustain ourselves according to the Ten Commandments of God.*[13]

Have the banning of prayer and Bible reading and the purging of the Ten Commandments in school had any measurable impact on society? David Barton's book. *To Pray Or Not To Pray*, uses government statistics to show what has happened. In 1963 the U.S. Supreme Court in *Engel v. Vitale* ruled that it was unconstitutional for school students to acknowledge their dependence on God and ask Him for His blessings. The "unconstitutional" prayer the students in New York state schools prayed to open school days said:

> *Almighty God, we acknowledge our dependence upon thee, and we beg Thy blessings upon us, our parents, our teachers, and our Country.*

Since the Supreme Court ruled that it was unconstitutional for students to say that prayer in school...

> *...the divorce rate in America has doubled....the rate of sexually transmitted diseases has jumped 250%....pre-marital teenage sex and pregnancies have doubled....Average scores on the SAT College entrance exams fell 80 points in the ten years after the students' prayer asking for God's blessings upon themselves and their teachers was ruled unconstitutional.*[14]

THE ACLU OPPOSES SCHOOL PRAYER

For almost fifty years the American Civil Liberties Union (ACLU) and attorneys associated with it have been involved in nearly every judicial attack on prayer in schools. The ACLU has also led fights against posting the Ten Commandments and other public recognitions of God in society. Chapter XI documents how since 1977, federal judges have awarded the ACLU multiplied millions of dollars in taxpayer money. The ACLU collects judge-awarded legal fees for filing federal civil rights suits. The ACLU represents people "offended" when hearing a prayer or when they have to see the Ten Commandments posted in a public place. That's how the ACLU gets millions of taxpayer dollars to finance its lawsuits against public recognition of God.

CONTROL OF ALL BUSINESS AND FARMS

As was mentioned earlier, anti-God, anti-morality court decisions are just the tip of a gigantic iceberg. Supreme Court decisions have repeatedly overturned the Constitution's limitations on the power of the federal government.

Supreme Court decisions have given the federal government control over wages, working conditions, and hiring and firing practices of most businesses. The judges also extended federal control over what farmers can plant in their fields. Article I, Section 8 of the Constitution gives the federal government authority to regulate commerce *between* the States. The Court has reinterpreted the Constitution's commerce clause to transfer jurisdiction over what had always been State functions from the States to the federal government, its courts and its bureaucrats. Two Supreme Court decisions show how it has been done. They illustrate what Jefferson called judicial "twisting and shaping" of the U.S. Constitution. During New Deal days in the 1930 and 1940s, for example, the Supreme Court stretched the definition of *interstate commerce* by ruling that...

> *...an elevator operator in a New Jersey office building who spent his days running his elevator from the first floor to the sixth floor was engaged in interstate commerce. The Supreme Court, in A.B. Kirschbaum v. Walling (1942) ruled that if a salesman from New York came to New Jersey to visit a prospective customer in a sixth floor office, he would use the elevator. The elevator operator was therefore engaged in interstate commerce and the federal government had the authority to regulate his wages and hours.* [15]

The decision, written by Justice Felix Frankfurter, established a far reaching precedent. It has been expanded to give the federal government and its bureaucracy almost total regulatory authority over all wages, hours, working conditions, overtime, hiring practices, etc. Almost all businesses in the United States have been effected.

Judges similarly used control of interstate commerce to give the federal government oversight and control over farms and farmers in the 1930s. Farm products such as wheat and corn, beef, pork, chickens and their eggs, milk, etc. sometimes move across state lines. Such moving of products *across state lines* is interstate commerce and is subject to control by Congress and federal bureaucrats. The Supreme Court applied that concept in this far-fetched way.

An Ohio farmer refused to submit to federal controls on the amount of grain he could plant on ten acres of his own ground. He argued that he never sold the grain so it wasn't in interstate commerce and therefore wasn't subject to federal control. The grain he produced was fed to animals and poultry on his farm. The livestock and poultry were used to feed his own family. On that basis, the farmer contended that there was no commerce involved. Therefore, the federal government had no authority to control what he planted and fed to his own animals which his family ate.

However, the Supreme Court in *Wickard v. Filburn (1942)* ruled that the farmer was subject to penalties for violating federal rules on how much grain he could plant. The Supreme Court justices "reasoned" that if the farmer had not fed the grain to his own animals which were then eaten by his own family, he would have needed to buy food *which may have moved across state lines*. Such action *may have affected interstate commerce*. The farmer was, therefore, subject to federal control on what he could plant and harvest on his own land to feed his own family.[16] This decision transferred another right of the people to Washington bureaucrats—breaching the "wall of separation" the founders created through the Constitution.

JUDICIAL CONTROL OF CRIMINAL JUSTICE

The Supreme Court also repeatedly intervenes in State administration of criminal justice. (Chapter VIII examines how traditional State authority over criminal justice has been transferred to

Washington's federal courts.) One recent illustration is sufficient here:

> *Triple-murderer David Larry Nelson was three hours from execution on Alabama's death row in 2004 after exhausting twenty years of appeals. The Supreme Court unanimously granted him another stay of execution in May 2004. Nelson claimed that executing him by legal injection would be "cruel and unusual punishment." Nelson said that because his veins had been damaged by his long time intravenous drug use, it would be impossible to insert the needle into his vein to inject the lethal drug without cutting deep into his flesh and muscle. Physicians supporting Nelson's appeal told the Court that done improperly the injection procedure could cause Nelson to hemorrhage and suffer heart problems before the lethal injection could kill him.[17]*

Justice Sandra Day O'Connor, writing for the Court, put a stay on the execution. Her decision said that Nelson should be allowed to argue that his punishment would be unconstitutionally cruel unless special precautions were taken.

Contrast the quickness with which the Supreme Court intervened in that case to protect a murderer from execution with its handling of the case of Terri Schiavo. Without any explanation, the Supreme Court refused five times in 2004 and 2005 to examine whether it could be a violation of the rights of the Florida woman to deny her all food and water. When judges in Florida and the Supreme Court refused to get involved, Terri Schiavo died an agonizing death from thirst, dehydration and starvation.[18]

The Supreme Court may have had some unstated legal basis for refusing to examine the Terri Schiavo case. It appears, however, to find far-fetched "reasons" for protecting the "rights" of convicted murderers. As a result, only a tiny fraction of those convicted of murder and sentenced to death are ever executed. If they are, the execution comes only after endless appeals. Convicted and sentenced murders stay on death row for fifteen or twenty years.

FREE SPEECH AND PORNOGRAPHY

For at least forty years, while the Court was supposedly defending free speech it has opened the door to distribution of pornography. The Child Online Protection Act (COPA) was passed by Congress in

1998. It was signed by President Clinton. No adult would have been restricted by COPA from viewing or purchasing on-line pornography. That had already been given 1st Amendment protection by the Supreme Court. However, COPA did require that Internet web sites be designed to limit children's access to pornography. On the closing day of the Court's 2003-2004 session it blocked enforcement of COPA. Justice Anthony Kennedy (who also wrote the decision to give constitutional protection to homosexual sodomy) said that if the COPA bill were enforced it has...

> ...a potential for extraordinary harm and a serious chill upon protected speech.[19]

Phyllis Schlafly in her July 14, 2004 column asked:

> Do you ever wonder why the Internet is so polluted with pornography? The Supreme Court just reminded us why: it blocks every attempt by Congress to regulate pornographers....For decades pornographers have enjoyed better treatment by our courts than any other industry. The justices have constitutionally protected obscenity in libraries, filth over cable television, and now unlimited INTERNET pornography....judges obsession with smut is astounding.[20]

The Court might be thought to be bending over backward to uphold the 1st Amendment's freedom of speech protections. However, the motives of the justices came into real question because of their December 2003 decision in *McConnell v. Federal Election Commission*.[21]

In that decision, the Court upheld the McCain-Feingold Campaign Finance law. That law severely limits the political speech of non-profit groups before an election. The 1st Amendment was written specifically to protect political speech. Even so, the Supreme Court, which protected the "freedom of speech" of pornographers, denied the free speech rights of public interest groups like the National Rifle Association or National Right-to-Life. Under McCain-Feingold they can't oppose or support candidates by name 60 days before an election.

The *Wall Street Journal* discussed the Court's McCain-Feingold decision. The editorial quoted the 1st Amendment which says "Congress shall make no law...abridging the freedom of speech." The editorial then commented...

> It says a lot about the power of those ten First Amendment words that it took the Supreme Court 298 pages of legal contortions this week to get around them. We'd have all been better off if the Court had simply taken a hint from the Founders and struck down campaign finance reform.... James Madison is surely turning in his grave.[22]

Justice Antonin Scalia in a McCain-Feingold withering dissent said:

> Who could have imagined that the same court which within the past four years has sternly disapproved of restrictions upon unconsequential forms of expression [pornography] would smile with favor upon a law which cuts to the heart of what the first amendment is meant to protect: The right of the people to criticize the government.

COURT USE OF FOREIGN PRECEDENTS

Those concerned about court decisions which have expanded the power of the federal government at the expense of the States, may not have seen anything yet. The U.S. Supreme Court now uses decisions of European nations and international commissions in changing the laws and practices of the United States and its States. Alan Sears, president of the Alliance Defense Fund, wrote:

> It's bad enough when judges legislate from the bench, but appealing to foreign courts for decisions to apply in our country, is in the minds of some, almost treasonous. Yet an appeal to share with a "wider civilization" was part of the reasoning used by the United States Supreme Court in its opinion in Lawrence v. Texas....It argued that "European nations have taken action" to favor homosexual behavior, and therefore the U.S. should also....In appealing to such precedents, the court may have laid the groundwork for more mischief down the road than most readers recognize.[23]

On ABC's This Week, Supreme Court Justice Stephen Breyer was interviewed by George Stephanopolous. Breyer said that a challenge for the next generation will be "whether our Constitution fits and how it fits into the governing documents of other nations."[24]

Phyllis Schlafly commented on Breyer's remarks, asking:

Where did Justice Breyer get the idea that the U.S. Constitution should "fit" into the laws of other nations? If a country can't make its own laws, how can it be a sovereign nation?[25]

Paul Craig Roberts, who served in the Reagan cabinet, recognizes the problem in the courts. In a June 17, 2001 *Washington Times* column he wrote:

American law schools should terminate their constitutional law courses, because the subject no longer exists. Judicial law has replaced constitutional law. Formerly, judges scrutinized legislation to ensure its conformity with the Constitution. Today judges are legislators themselves, and there is no branch of government to hold judicial legislation accountable to the Constitution.

Even one comedian acknowledged the problem. When the U.S. started looking for a way to help Iraq establish self-government, late-night TV host Jay Leno said:

They keep talking about drafting a constitution for Iraq. Why don't we just give them ours? It was written by a lot of really smart guys; it's worked for over 200 years; and we're not using it anymore.[26]

What can be done? Dr. D. James Kennedy concluded a Coral Ridge Ministries Television Special on runaway judges with these words:

When we the people care enough, with God's help we can prevail. We need not be slaves to our out of control courts. We need not live under the tyranny of judges. We cannot stand silently by.[27]

President Abraham Lincoln addressed the danger of rule by judges in his first inaugural address. He said:

If the policy of the government upon vital questions affecting the whole people is to be irrevocably fixed by decisions of the Supreme Court, the people will cease to be their own rulers.

How can "people" reclaim their right to self rule? How can legal foundations destroyed by court decisions be rebuilt? For years, "people" and groups have lobbied, without success, for constitutional amendments and laws to repair the damage done by the Supreme Court. They have sought to restore the Constitutional foundations for morality and the freedom of the individual and his property. But they have made these efforts without knowing and understanding the basis from which traditional freedoms came. Therefore, they have largely failed. As the years have passed, frustration and, sometimes, despair has resulted. What is the real answer?

When Americans say the Pledge of Allegiance to the flag, they affirm that the United States was founded as "One nation under God." They may be sincere in reciting those words. But few really know and understand that the United States was built on a very different foundation than that of any other nation in history. Few truly recognize and understand the importance of the truth that our nation, our courts, our government structure and our freedoms were based on God and His Word.

How did that foundation develop?

After the printing press was invented, the Bible started to be translated and published in the language of the people. In about 1500 A.D. Bible truths became the foundation of what is known today as western civilization. For the next 200 years, men in England, France and America studied, speculated and debated. They studied to see what the Bible revealed about God and government. The *Declaration of Independence* developed from those efforts.

Our founding fathers discovered and set forth the truth that God, the Creator, is the ultimate sovereign authority for individuals, for nations and for their governments as well. They recognized that rights come, not from a king, a government, a Constitution nor the Bill of Rights, but from God. The Declaration set forth this truth. The Constitution was written to "secure these rights" by restraining government from interfering with man's God-given rights.

These are foundational truths. Because schools (and too many churches) no longer teach them, our government, our courts, our Congress, our culture and our way of life have been transformed. It has happened because God, as the next chapter shows, is no longer recognized as the ultimate and final authority by most individuals.

Calvin Coolidge was the 30th President of the United States. He recognized and spoke out regularly on the influence of the Bible and Christianity as the foundation for American freedom. Coolidge is quoted as having said:

America was born in a revival of religion. Back of that revival were John Wesley, George Whitefield, and Francis Asbury.[28]

In his autobiography, Benjamin Franklin provides his eyewitness account of how God worked. During that revival in the 1740-1775 period God changed men's hearts. Changed men then worked to change the whole face of America. When George Whitefield came to America, 31-year old Ben Franklin was among the multitudes who thronged to hear him preach in the churches and in the streets. In his writings, Franklin expressed amazement at the "extraordinary influence" Whitefield's words had on the crowds. He had this influence, Franklin said, "notwithstanding his common abuse of them that they were naturally beasts and devils."[29]

Whitefield's goal, of course, was to show men that in God's sight all are sinners. They are incapable of making themselves good enough for God. Those who came to see that they had no righteousness of their own to offer God were ready to hear the good news of the Gospel. Whitefield then proclaimed the love of the God who sent His sinless Son, Jesus Christ, to suffer and die on the Cross to pay the penalty for the sins of mankind. Whitefield pled with sinners to believe that Christ had died for them personally. Seeing that, they might then individually invite the Risen Christ into their hearts to be Lord and Savior. This was the simple and supernatural message that transformed America in the thirty years before the War for Independence. Ben Franklin never told of responding personally, but he reported:

It was wonderful to see the change soon made in the manners of our inhabitants. From being thoughtless or indifferent about religion, it seems as if all the world were growing religious, so that one could not walk thro' the town in an evening without hearing psalms sung in different families of every street.[30]

That describes revival. That was the atmosphere in which America was born. Out of it our government, our courts and our system of law were formed.

When George Whitefield preached in Boston twenty-two preachers were converted. Even Harvard University was affected. Before Whitefield came to Boston, the president of Harvard wrote to a friend complaining of the moral decay in the college, He said:

*Whence is there such a prevalancy of so many immoralities
amongst the professors? Why so little success of the Gospel?*[31]

Later, describing the revival which came to the Harvard campus,
President Willard wrote:

*That which forebodes the most lasting advantage is the new state
of the college. Gentlemen's sons that were sent here only for a mere
polite education, are now so full of zeal for the cause of Christ and
the love of souls as to devote themselves absolutely to the study of
divinity. The college is entirely changed; the students are full of
God—and will I hope come out blessings to this and succeeding
generations.*[32]

Some of the founding fathers were among those students who
heard Whitefield preach in 1739. Others were students of the signer
of the Declaration John Witherspoon at Princeton. In those days,
future lawyers studied in seminaries.

President Calvin Coolidge, whose statement that America was
born in a revival was quoted earlier, added:

*The foundations of our society and our government rest so much
on the teachings of the Bible that it would be difficult to support
them if faith in these teachings would cease to be practically
universal in our country.*[33]

That has now happened. The nation has turned away from God.
Succeeding chapters of this book will spell out just how the Bible
and men's understanding of it influenced the development of our
courts and our system of law. Chapter V will examine foreign
academic philosophies which developed in the 19th century. Those
anti-God philosophies have influenced and changed schools and
universities, the government, and the courts. Too many churches
and their people have been affected also. Understanding this history
is the key to rebuilding the foundations destroyed by judges and
courts. That is the goal and purpose of this book.

America's Biblical foundation, her *Declaration of Independence,*
and her Constitution have been betrayed. Law schools, law practitioners, and many judges—from the lowest courts to those who sit
on the bench of the Supreme Court—no longer uphold standards of
morality and decency based on the Founding Fathers' intent and
vision. America must return to her roots, and soon.

It is important to oppose court decisions and philosophies which opened the door to abortion, sodomy and the homosexual "lifestyle." It is important to resist the transfer of the right of self-government from the States and the people to Washington. However, as important as these efforts are, none can be successful apart from a revival of the religion of Jesus Christ. It must be a revival of the sort which transformed America in the 1700s. From that revival came the *Declaration of Independence*, the Constitution and the structure of the federal/State government they produced. The next several chapters examine much of that history which is now denied or forgotten.

Understanding where we once were and how we have gotten to where we are today, can be used to bring America back to again being truly "One nation under God." For it to happen, concerned people must realize that nations don't turn from God and nations can't turn to God. Only individuals can. The Bible spells out the only way individuals can turn to God. In the New Testament Gospel of John, the Lord Jesus said:

I am the way, the truth, and the life: no man cometh unto the Father, but by me. (John 14:6)

He could make that claim. He is the one who died for the sins of all, was buried and was raised again from the dead to be the new life of those who believe.

In the Old Testament, II Chronicles 7:14, God promises:

If my people, which are called by my name, shall humble themselves. and pray, and seek my face, and turn from their wicked way; then will I hear from heaven, and will forgive their sin, and will heal their land.

This book challenges you to participate in that effort.

John Stormer
Florissant, Missouri
July 2005

*Constitution: A set of fundamental principles
for the government of rational and social beings.
—Noah Webster, 1828 Dictionary*

CHAPTER I

WHAT HAS HAPPENED
TO CONSTITUTIONAL AWARENESS
AND RESPECT?

If we'd really go back to applying the Constitution as it was written, there are all sorts of things that we in government won't be able to do.
        —*Missouri State Senator Jerry Howard, 1996*

FORMER MISSOURI STATE SENATOR JERRY HOWARD is unusual among Americans. He apparently understood the strong limitations that the Constitution applies to the government and its activities. Senator Howard appeared before a district meeting of the Missouri Farm Bureau in 1996 where candidates were being interviewed. Howard, a state senator, was being challenged for reelection. His opponent pledged to work to return the nation and its government to constitutional foundations. Howard ridiculed his opponent's desire and appealed to the Farm Bureau audience saying, "...going back to a strict interpretation of the Constitution, and a strict implementation of the 10th amendment, would mean that we wouldn't be able to do some of the farm programs."[1] His opponent said, "Amen," and commented that a lot more than farm programs were involved. The opponent received the endorsement.

Senator Howard, like many others, had repeatedly taken the oath to uphold the Constitution during his military service and his twenty-five years in the Missouri legislature

Most citizens and even those in political office do not have the understanding of the U.S. Constitution that Senator Howard's statement seem to display. The understanding that the Constitution was written to severely limit the activities and authority of the federal government has been largely lost.

All who serve in the military, on police forces, local school boards and city councils, or in state and federal offices take an oath of office. They swear to support and uphold the U.S. Constitution. Few of them apparently know what it really says and what it was written to do. Many who swear to uphold it have never read it.

In fact, attorneys and judges who have really read and studied the Constitution itself are a rarity. During a two year period, the author of this book surveyed every attorney and judge he met. They were asked the following questions:

(1.) When you were in law school did you take a class in Constitutional law?

All answered, "Yes." Some groaned and volunteered that the textbook was several inches thick. After displaying my pocket Constitution, I asked:

(2.) When you took your Constitutional law class, did you, in class, actually read and study the Constitution itself? Or did you just study Supreme Court decisions which told you what to believe about the Constitution?

More than 100 attorneys and judges were questioned over a two year period. Only two of them reported actually reading and studying the Constitution in their Constitutional Law classes. One went to Oral Roberts Law School. The other went to Pat Robertson's Regent Law School several years later. Herb Titus was the Constitutional Law professor both places. Some of those surveyed who did not actually study the Constitution in law school said, "I studied it on my own so I could bug the liberal professors."

CONSTITUTION GETS JUDGE IN TROUBLE

I asked Alabama's *Ten Commandments Judge*, Roy Moore, the questions in April 2000. He laughed and said, "Seven or eight years ago as a sitting judge I came to realize that I knew very little about the Constitution. I started to study it on my own, and I've been in trouble ever since."

Roy Moore was elected as Chief Justice of the Alabama Supreme Court in 2001. Two years later he was removed from office for acknowledging God in the performance of his duties. A full discussion of his case, the orders of the federal judge and the proceedings of the Court of the Judiciary which dismissed Moore are examined in Chapter IX.

I started asking attorneys and judges about whether they had ever read and studied the Constitution as a result of a meeting in September 1999 with the then Texas Governor, George W. Bush. I was one of a small group of conservative Christians which spent six months in 1999 quietly interviewing most of the Republican presidential candidates.

During a two hour face-to-face meeting with then Governor Bush, I had an opportunity to ask one question. It is the question at the top of my list when evaluating candidates. Reading from my pocket copy of the United States Constitution, I said:

Governor Bush, when you are elected President next year, you will be asked to swear that you will, to the best of your ability, preserve, protect and defend the Constitution of the United States.

Bush nodded agreement. I then added:

In preserving, protecting and defending the Constitution, would you see it as your duty to veto any and all appropriations which would finance any federal activity which is unconstitutional?

Quickly, I added:

That's rather broad, so I'll narrow it down. Would you, for example, veto appropriations for the federal Department of Education and for the National Endowment for the Arts? [That is the group which has used taxpayer money to finance as art, a crucifix in urine and cow dung on a picture of the Virgin Mary.]

Bush smiled, shuffled and then asked:

How could we know what's unconstitutional?

I pointed out that Article I, Section 8 of the Constitution specifically spells out the areas in which Congress can legislate and the federal government can operate. Financing art and controlling public education are not among them. Bush did some more rambling and concluded by saying:

Well, in some things you just have to be practical.

At the conclusion of the meeting, Bush who is very personable, came to me, smiled, shook my hand, and said, "That was a very good question you asked. I just didn't know how to handle it."

At the time I was shocked. Since then I've had to realize that Bush's position was basically the same as that of almost every president for at least 75 years. Based on their voting records, almost every member of Congress, with a few exceptions, has had the same attitude toward the Constitution. That's why the nation is in the mess it is in politically, economically, socially and internationally. The efforts of one Congressman to awaken his Congressional colleagues to the need for a real return to Constitutional government is discussed in Chapter XIII.

Even many staunchly conservative members of Congress have no understanding of the Constitution. That is why they get entrapped into supporting many unconstitutional "compromises." They do it to achieve what they see as *"a good end"* or as *"a moving in the right direction."* A friend of over twenty years is a good example. After service in his state legislature, he was elected to Congress in the early 1990s. I knew that while he was a committed Christian and a conservative, he was not a Constitutionalist. I just didn't realize at the time how serious that was. In Washington, he regularly compiled a 90% conservative voting record. But on some key issues like most "conservatives," he would go astray on a critical vote.

I arranged to meet with him after he had been in Washington for several years. To lay the foundation for what I wanted to discuss, I established that he believed the Bible was the inspired, in errant, infallible Word of God. We further agreed that God had every word in the Bible written just as He wanted it written. That being so, the Bible shouldn't be reinterpreted to "meet the needs of today." Many liberal churches, seminaries, etc. reject that truth today. But, the Congressman and I were in agreement that the Bible shouldn't be reinterpreted to fit into today's culture.

I then tried to get him to apply the same thinking to the Constitution. I said, "The Founding Fathers wrote specific language. They intended for it to be applied in just the way they wrote it. They sometimes debated for days over whether or not to include some word or specific provision. They knew that words had meaning."

Several of them wrote the *Federalist Papers* to explain what they said and how it should be understood and applied. The Founders did recognize that as history unfolded in the future, changes in conditions might make some changes necessary. That's why they included the amendment process in Article V.

From that foundation, I added, "Therefore, the Constitution should be understood, interpreted and applied based on just what the original words meant."

My friend said, "No, you have to understand that the Constitution is a living document which has evolved to meet the needs of people today." He is a graduate of a prestigious law school, generally regarded to be conservative.

At that point perhaps I wasn't very nice. In an attempt to make him see the fallacy and the danger in his position, I asked, "What do you see as the proper function of government today?" He replied:

Government is the agency through which we get the power to meet the needs of the people.

I perhaps put a friend in an unkind place when I replied to his answer with this comment:

In other words, it appears that although you are a conservative, you have the same philosophy of government as Teddy Kennedy. However, you see some of the needs of the people differently than he does.

This conservative member of Congress is not unusual. He is the product of what the schools of America have been doing to at least three generations of American children. They are the people who are now voters, serve in Congress and sit as judges in the courts.

FEW KNOW PROPER ROLE OF GOVERNMENT

Very few voters, whether "conservative" or "liberal," have any idea of the proper role of government. Few have any understanding that our federal government under the Constitution was established with very limited functions. Those included "making secure" the rights given to Americans by God and protecting Americans from foreign enemies and from each other. There is no seeming understanding of those truths. Too many voters today believe government was established to provide "things" and services for them. As a result, both parties promise all things to all people.

People have come to this position because several generations of American young people have been trained and conditioned to believe it by America's schools.

Most states require that students be taught and tested on the U.S. Constitution. For the most part schools have been doing a poor job for years. Students may learn that the Constitution establishes a federal government with three branches. It is unlikely, however, that students are taught that Article 1, Section 8 of the Constitution only authorizes the Congress and the federal government to legislate and act in about twenty specific areas. Those specific areas do not include any federal involvement in a whole host of present activities. Education, subsidizing the National Endowment for the Arts (which finances "art" including a crucifix immersed in a jar of urine) and a host of other inane activities cost the money of taxpayers. They have no Constitutional authority. Violating Constitutional limitations has worked the hand of government into the lives and businesses of every American. Some areas into which the federal government has moved may be functions which are needed. However, they are unconstitutional if not specifically authorized in that document or in amendments to it.

TWO KEY AMENDMENTS IGNORED

Few Americans today were taught in school the importance of the Ninth and Tenth Amendments to the Constitution. Those amendments reserve for the states and the people all those rights and powers not *specifically* given to the federal government. To limit the federal government in this way is why the states and the people wrote the Constitution.

Schools don't just fail to give students a true understanding of the *Declaration of Independence* and the Constitution. Textbooks in widespread use in the schools of America for the last fifty years have taught that the Constitution, as written, is no longer practical. It must be changed, the books say, not by amendment, but by judicial interpretation. The book, *None Dare Call It Education*, written by the author of this book documents how it has been done. It quotes illustration after illustration from public school textbooks.

F. A. Magruder's *American Government,* for example, has been widely used in schools for over 50 years. The 1952 edition openly admits that important constitutional safeguards were being bypassed then as they are today. The student is given the impression that erosion of constitutional guarantees against an all-powerful government is "sophisticated and progressive." In 1952, Magruder's textbook told students:

> *The principle of checks and balances in government is not held in such esteem today as it was a century ago. The people no longer fear officers they elect every few years.*[2]

Magruder doesn't point out that the people of Germany didn't "fear" Hitler after they elected him in 1933. Therefore, they ignored the checks and balances written into the German constitution. They allowed Hitler to assume more and more power. As a result the people of Germany never had an opportunity to vote him out. Students are not warned that it could happen here or in any country unless government is bound by the "chains" of its Constitution.

Guided class discussions are used cleverly in schools to bring generations of students to believe the Constitution is outmoded. The teacher's manual for the McGraw-Hill/Webster Division 1980 high school text, *American Government* tells teachers to start a discussion of "OUR LIVING CONSTITUTION" this way:

> *...ask students whether they would consider going to a dentist...[or] use a doctor who practiced medicine as it was practiced in the thirteen colonies?...ask them how they manage to live under a United States Constitution that is 200 years old. Is that Constitution as out of date as the dental and medical techniques of 200 years ago?*[3]

AN EVOLVING, LIVING CONSTITUTION?

Such "guided" discussions condition students to see the "wisdom" of ignoring or reinterpreting much of the "outmoded" Constitution. The Constitution is then pictured as "a living document." It is being "evolved" by today's wise judges to meet today's problems. That's a far cry from what our founders envisioned. Even so, the author of the 1991 Houghton-Mifflin eighth grade social studies text, *A More Perfect Union* tells students:

> *The Constitution is not a rigid document. Because of imprecise language in some sections, it is <u>open to interpretation.</u> Most historians feel that this is more of a strength than a weakness. A level of interpretation is ensured, while another level can be <u>reinterpreted by successive generations.</u> ...By <u>unofficial [change]</u>*

method is meant...the Supreme Court's interpretation...which differs sometimes depending on the views of new justices[4] (Emphasis added.)

Anthony Kennedy was nominated to serve on the U.S. Supreme Court by Ronald Reagan. Kennedy was considered to be a staunch conservative. An indication that he wasn't could have been suspected during his confirmation hearing. He affirmed that he was firmly committed to the concept that the Constitution was "a living document." On the Court, of course, Kennedy has written decision after decision which has turned the Constitution upside down. He wrote the 2003 decision which legalized the practice of sodomy.[5] The decision overturned previous Supreme Court decisions and the laws of Texas and other states. The *Lawrence v. Texas* decision "found" a new constitutional right to practice sodomy. The decision resulted from the "principle" that the Constitution is a "living" document. In other words, its basic meaning *evolves* over time as society changes rather than being "stuck" on some 18th century understanding of morals.

Kennedy is not alone in adhering to his belief that the Constitution is a "living" document. During the 2000 presidential primary, Vice President Gore was asked what type of Supreme Court justices he would appoint. Gore said:

I would look for justices of the Supreme Court who understand that our Constitution is a living, breathing document, that it was intended by our Founders to be interpreted in the light of the constantly evolving experience of the American people.[6]

In his 1990 book, *The Tempting of America: The Political Seduction of the Law,* Judge Robert Bork summed up where the "Living Constitution" concept has taken us. He said:

The abandonment of original understanding in modern times means the transportation into the Constitution of principles of a liberal culture that cannot achieve those results democratically....Either the Constitution and statutes are law, which means their principles are known and control judges, or they are malleable texts that judges may rewrite to see that particular groups or causes win....When we speak of "law," we ordinarily refer to a rule that we have no right to change except through prescribed proce-

dures. That statement assumes that the rule has meaning independent of our own desires.[7]

Justice Antonin Scalia believes that the Constitution should be read and interpreted in accordance with the original intent of the Founders. As to whether the Constitution lives and grows, Scalia has said:

The Constitution is not an organism. It is a legal document.[8]

One commentator wrote:

A "living" Constitution grows and changes with the times. Generally speaking, liberals want a living Constitution and conservatives don't.

Harvard Law School professor Alan Dershowitz supports a living constitution. In the October 2004 *American Legion Magazine*, Dershowitz defined the question asking:

Should these words, written years earlier, be constantly reinterpreted to address current problems and current needs? Or should they mean precisely what those who wrote them intended them to mean?[9]

In the same magazine, David Barton, author of *Original Intent: The Courts, The Constitution and Religion,* puts the controversy in a meaningful context. He says:

Under the "living" constitution approach, history and precedent are largely irrelevant. Instead, unelected judges create policy to reflect modern needs through the constitution they themselves write.[10]

This isn't just the judgment of Barton, a conservative. The words of former Chief Justice Charles Evans Hughes quoted in the introduction validate Barton's conclusion and they bear repeating. Hughes said it all when he said:

We are under a constitution, but the constitution is what the judges say it is.[11]

In other words, there are no absolutes. The Constitution changes anytime judges decide to change it.

Dershowitz approvingly quotes Supreme Court Justice Ruth Bader Ginsburg and others who believe that the living constitution approach "expands rights beyond its original narrow purview....evolving toward more liberty." Those who have lost their rights to pray, read the Bible, post the Ten Commandments, or plant fields free of government control through court decisions might question whether their "rights" have been expanded by "living constitution" judges.

Two months after *The American Legion Magazine* printed the Dershowitz/Barton "debate," letter writers responded. An Allendale, Michigan man, R. Douglas McCrea wrote:

> *"A Tale of Two Constitutions" disturbed me so badly that I had to reread the Declaration of Independence and the Constitution....after reading both documents, it occurred to me that allowing the "evolving" theory to go on is tantamount to begging a tyranny of the judiciary. The question now is how to stop it.*[12]

The letter of Les Balty of Jefferson City, Missouri said:

> *You gave a balanced report on the two constitutional viewpoints, but the "evolving document" view is the road to tyranny. We are already subject to dictators in robes. Federal judges who abuse their power are simply unelected, appointed for life dictators. For what is a dictatorship but the majority ruled by a few. Our democratic republic has been in peril for decades.*[13]

Tom Edwards of Matador, Texas responded to the magazine debate, with real insight, saying:

> *Undergirding each [method of constitutional interpretation] is a philosophical assumption about the nature of truth. A relativist assumes that there are no absolute truths and that all is evolving, ultimately, to perfection. An absolutist recognizes certain absolutes, including moral, and that in this instance some are embodied in the Constitution. Dershowitz takes a relativist approach and is a master at making the absurd sound reasonable, whereas Barton joins the founders in believing in absolute "self-evident truths." ....To reinterpret the Constitution to mirror our devolving society corrupts the document and it ceases to be one.*[14]

An educational researcher, Michael J. Chapman, did an exhaustive review of the Houghton-Mifflin eighth grade textbook quoted earlier. That was the textbook which advocates a "flexible constitution." Chapman summed up the problem. He showed that when a textbook tells students that the Constitution could be reinterpreted by successive generations, it conditions them to accept the concept of a "living, changing Constitution." Chapman concluded:

> *Children are being taught that moral-relativism is a virtue built into our Constitution. Without accountability to absolute law, legislation is vaguely written and then left up to the courts to define "depending on the views of new justices."*[15]

Thomas Jefferson foresaw this possibility and warned future justices about the danger. On June 12, 1823 he wrote to Justice William Johnson:

> *On every question of construction, carry yourselves back to the time when the Constitution was adopted, recollect the spirit manifested in the debates, and instead of trying what meaning may be squeezed out of the text, or invented against it, conform to the probable one in which it was passed.*[16]

The *Elementary Textbook Evaluation Guide* was published in 1961 by the Textbook Study League Inc. of San Gabriel, California. It warned of the ultimate result of ignoring God as the source of an individual's rights. It said:

> *Withhold from the children for one generation the truth of "rights endowed by the Creator" and our Constitution could be altered and our freedom could be voted away without citizens ever knowing the cause of their slavery.*[17]

Those words are basically a paraphrase of the words of Thomas Jefferson, the author of the Declaration, who said:

> *God who gave us life gave us liberty. Can the liberties of a nation be secure when we have removed a conviction that these liberties are the gift of God? Indeed I tremble for my country when I reflect that God is just, that His justice cannot sleep forever.*[18]

Generations of children have not been given a true understanding of the Biblical basis for our freedoms and liberty. They grow up to become teachers, voters, state representatives, members of Congress, Supreme Court justices and presidents.

How will the failure to give succeeding generations of Americans an understanding of the nation's Constitutional foundations affect the future? An incident which happened a month before the November 2000 election gives insight. The author of this book spent a week in Vermont working with legislative candidates who were opposing same sex unions. The Vermont legislature, under an order of the Vermont Supreme Court, had *legalized* same sex unions earlier in 2000. Opponents of same-sex unions won enough seats in the 2000 election to take control of the Vermont House of Representatives.

However, such victories by an aroused people may be only temporary. While in Vermont, I campaigned with a candidate for the Vermont Senate. A supporter of same sex unions rather defiantly told us, "You people may win in November, but you better realize that your children will end up voting you out of office." That vocal advocate for the "lifestyle" that demands same sex unions knows what schools are doing to America's children. He knows what the ultimate result could be.

A foreshadowing of what schools may have "children" doing in the future was shown by a group of ninth grade Vermont students in early 2004. They petitioned the Vermont Senate Operations committee to remove all references to Almighty God and Christianity from the Vermont Constitution. The students were granted a hearing before the Senate committee on January 30, 2004. The next day the Barre/Montpelier, Vermont *Times Argus* told the story.[19]

> *A fourteen year old young lady, in her testimony, advocated the removal of references to Almighty God and Christianity from the Vermont Constitution. She told the committee that in the age of diversity in which we live having such words in the Constitution is an "anachronistic embarrassment." (Quite a vocabulary for a 14-year old.)*

The passages in the Vermont Constitution, which the students found embarrassing and want changed, guarantee freedom of religion. They read...

> *...all persons shall have a natural and unalienable right, to worship Almighty God, according to the dictates of their own consciences and understandings, as in their opinion shall be regulated by the word of God....every sect or denomination of Christians ought to observe the sabbath or Lord's day, and keep some sort of religious worship, which to them shall seem most agreeable to the revealed will of God.*[20]

That passage from the Vermont Constitution recognizes Almighty God as Someone to be worshipped. It points Christians to worshiping on the Lord's Day. The Constitution also recognizes that God reveals His will through His Word. Those are not acceptable concepts in a day of *political correctness.* To some students they are "an embarrassment in a day of diversity."

Students at Twinfield Union High School in Plainfield, Vermont embarked on their project to remove God from the Vermont Constitution as a part of a national civics education program called "Project Citizen."[21] In that program, middle school (7th and 8th grade) students study ways of influencing public policy. In class they formulate a goal for making a change they agree upon. They then develop a program for getting the change made. That's how a year later the Vermont students ended up with a hearing before the Senate Governmental Operations Committee.

The "Project Citizen" program which motivated the Vermont students was created by the Center for Civic Education, 5146 Douglas Fir Rd, Calabasas CA 91302. It is a non-governmental organization (NGO). When Congress passed HR6 in 1994 the CCE was given the responsibility *and the finances* for developing the national curriculum for civic education in the United States.[22] CCE supplies textbooks and guidance widely without charge to any school (public or private) which agrees to use the program. The goal is making real activists of the students. That can be a good goal. However, there can be a danger in challenging and training young people to be "activists" if they have not already been given a knowledge and understanding of America's foundations and heritage. The direction in which students will be challenged to work will depend on the interests and any bias of the teacher. A teacher who is knowledgeable and discerning can use the program effectively. The Center for Civic Education textbook, *We The People: The Citizen and the Constitution,* is supplied to schools which request it. It gives an overview of history, the development of the Constitution, etc. The text mentions the *Declaration of Independence* several times but it never discusses or explains the concept in it that sets the United States apart from all other nations. That is the truth that the rights of Americans come from God. It never presents the viewpoint that the *Declaration of Independence* is key to correctly understanding and interpreting the Constitution.

The United States was founded as a nation under the God of the Bible, as the introductory chapter demonstrated. It was, therefore, a Christian nation. Without that understanding and history, students can be activated, as the Vermont students were. They demanded that Almighty God, His revealing of His will through the scriptures and Christianity be removed from the Vermont Constitution.

In its closing chapters, the CCE book, *We The People: The Citizen and the Constitution,* opens the door to discussions on how internationalism will affect American citizens. Students, for example, discuss the need to give resident aliens the right to vote on some issues, etc.[23] The importance of protecting national sovereignty isn't given attention. (The CCE program is financed by the U.S. taxpayers.)

The long range effect of creating activists before they have the right foundation was the basis for the pre-election remark made by the pro-homosexual activist in Vermont in 2000. Referring to those who worked for traditional values, he said, "You may win the election this time, but your kids will vote you out of office in the future." He knew the kind of activists the schools and their textbooks are creating.

To reverse that trend, traditional values Americans need to learn or relearn the foundational truths about America. Abortion, homosexuality, same sex marriages and whether or not schools can have prayer or post the Ten Commandments are just "symptoms" of the problem. The "symptoms" should be opposed but to do it effectively, Americans need to learn and understand what sets the United States apart from other nations. To be effective, citizens must know the basis for America's government, its courts and its justice system. These historic truths are set forth, discussed and explained in the chapters that follow. Once they are mastered personally, they must then be taught to coming generations, first on a one-to-one basis in our families. Ultimately the schools of the nation must be recaptured and used again to train all young people in the true basis of freedom.

CHAPTER II

TO UNDERSTAND THE CONSTITUTION
START WITH THE DECLARATION

The virtue which had been infused into the Constitution of the United States...was no other than...those abstract principles which had been first proclaimed in the Declaration of Independence—namely the self-evident truths of the natural and unalienable rights of man...and the sovereignty of the people, always subordinate to the rule of right and wrong, and always responsible to the Supreme Ruler of the universe for the rightful exercise of that power. <u>This was the platform upon which the Constitution of the United States had been erected.</u>[1]

—*President John Quincy Adams*

UNDERSTANDING THE ROLE of the *Declaration of Independence* in America's founding is the key to interpreting the Constitution correctly. To do so it is necessary to see how the purpose of the Declaration has a parallel in law today. The parallel is shown in this example:

When a new body or group (a business, church, not-for-profit group, etc.) is formed, Articles of Incorporation are written by the participating parties and made public when filed with the state. Those articles of incorporation set forth who is forming the group, the purpose and function of the body being formed, the activities in which it may engage, its name and its duration.[2]

The *Declaration of Independence* fulfilled those functions and became, in effect, the Articles of Incorporation for the United States.

Articles of incorporation are written and filed to establish an organization, business, etc. The group then writes a constitution and by-laws to spell out how the purposes as set forth in articles of incorporation will be carried out. In law, the constitution and by-laws and activities of an organization cannot go beyond the purposes set forth in its articles of incorporation. To do so can result in the organization losing its corporate charter and its right to operate. The Declaration established the United States. It authorized writing the Constitution to spell out how the new nation would function.

The U.S. Constitution was written to establish the procedures for making *secure* the rights given by God. That was the purpose set forth in the *Declaration of Independence*. The United States was the name the colonies took for themselves in the Declaration. The Declaration also said the new nation would continue as long as it fulfilled its purpose. The Declaration covered the four principle requirements for articles of incorporation.

A number of years ago, I was on a Christian school convention program. A justice on that State's Supreme Court was another participant. We ate breakfast together. I laid out to him the theory that the Declaration was, in effect, America's Articles of Incorporation and that the Constitution was written to implement how the purposes of the new nation would be fulfilled. He agreed. Then I added, "That being true, and using the same logic, any law, court decision or even an amendment to the Constitution itself which would violate the principles of the Declaration would be null and void." He said, "Oh no, you can't go that far."

However, a seed had been planted. As we ate dinner together that evening, he said "I've been thinking about what you proposed at breakfast. You are right—but if you try to argue that in court you'll lose. There must be a real job of re-educating the American people on the foundations of our freedom." That's one purpose of this book. Continually raising the issue in court would be another important step in the education process.

As we have seen, understanding the relationship between the Declaration and the Constitution is essential to properly interpreting and applying the Constitution. Such understanding should also produce a big question which should be being raised in court, in the media and in our churches and schools. The question was stated earlier. It is:

> *If as the Declaration of Independence declares, the U.S. Constitution was written to make "secure" our God-given rights, how can any court find in the Constitution "rights" to abort babies, engage in sodomy or have same sex unions—all actions which violate God's law? Would God give such rights?*

Tragically, however, much of society either doesn't know or has chosen to deny that the *Declaration of Independence* is America's foundational document.

For example, in May 2003, the Minnesota legislature, in a revolutionary action, initially rejected the National Curriculum for schools. That national curriculum had been mandated by President Clinton's *Goals 2000* and President Bush's *No Child Left Behind*. A real battle developed when the legislature started developing replacement standards for Minnesota schools. The version developed in the Minnesota House of Representatives mandated that schools...

...promote and preserve the principles contained in the Declaration of Independence.

That mandate was missing from the final version produced by the joint education committee. Senator Michelle Bachmann (R) addressed Senator Steve Kelley (D), the chairman and an attorney, and asked, "Why?" On the video of the session made at the time, Kelley responded:

Senator Bachmann, the Declaration of Independence has no legal status in defining people's rights and privileges.[3]

That is the basic position today of most history and government texts, law school textbooks, etc.

Ignoring or downgrading the Declaration shows up even in the works of those who want to restore the Constitution. Robert Bork is a staunch supporter of using the original intent of the writers in interpreting the Constitution. In his excellent book, *Slouching Towards Gomorrah* Bork decries the cultural subversion in America, much of it resulting from court decisions. Even so, in the past Bork has not advocated that the Declaration should be used in interpreting the Constitution. Bork has held that only the Constitution's actual words be considered.

Another example from a different perspective is Randy E. Barnett's fascinating book, *Restoring the Lost Constitution.*[4.] Barnett, a professor at the Boston University School of Law, is a libertarian. He documents in a valuable way how U.S. Supreme Court decisions have chopped "holes" in the Constitution. In the

preface of his book Barnett lists numerous classic cases supporting
his premise and adds:

> *In countless other opinions, the Supreme Courts justices affirmed
> they meant it when they said the Constitution did not mean what
> it apparently said.*[5]

In his first chapter Barnett gives a classic view for the purpose of
the Constitution. He writes:

> *The Constitution that was actually enacted and formally
> amended creates islands of government powers in a sea of liberty.*[6]

In other words, the Constitution as written sees man is free except
for certain specific grants of power to government. Barnett then
shows the result of what the Court has done over the years. He adds:

> *The judicially redacted constitution creates islands of liberty
> rights in a sea of governmental powers.*

Barnett is a strong supporter of individual rights and liberty.
However, he does not acknowledge that the Declaration or God is
the source of those rights. The eight-page index in his book does not
list the *Declaration of Independence* even once.

Barnett believes that all people, as human beings, are born with
natural rights which he calls "liberty rights." Barnett interprets and
applies the Constitution, as written, on what he calls *a presumption
of liberty*. That means that a right is presumed to exist unless it is
specifically denied in the Constitution. He bases much of that
premise on the Ninth Amendment to the Constitution. His approach
is interesting but opens the door for almost unlimited "rights," some
of which the God of Creation would not give. Barnett ignores the
Declaration of Independence and God as the source of the rights of
an individual. Therefore, he has argued cases supporting rights of
individuals to abort babies or smoke marijuana. These are "rights"
which the God of the Bible would not give.

James McClellan is usually regarded as a constitutional conservative. He discusses the Declaration in his valuable book, *Liberty,
Order and Justice—An Introduction to the Constitutional Principles
of American Government*.[7] However, he devotes 16 pages in his
otherwise valuable book to undermining the importance of the
Declaration.

McClellan does acknowledge that...

...The Declaration of Independence is one of the most famous documents in the history of the world and from its inception has exerted a powerful influence on mankind....and has become such a basic ingredient of the American political tradition as to be regarded by some as almost a part of the Constitution itself. (Pg. 122)

After those nice words, McClellan then undermines the Declaration. He says it has been a source of profound disagreements because...

...the first part of the Declaration, the preamble...is obscured by vague and ambiguous language that is susceptible to different interpretations. (Pg. 124)

Anyone who reads those first two paragraphs and has any background or understanding of the words used would question McClellan's statement about vagueness. As an example of the vagueness, McClellan asks:

Is the reference in the document to the "laws of nature" anything more than political rhetoric? (pg. 124)

McClellan's disparaging question appears to contradict his earlier statement that...:

...about half (of the signers) had been judges or lawyers who were deeply read in Sir William Blackstone's monumental treatise Commentaries on the Laws of England. (pg. 32-33)

If the founders were so knowledgeable in Blackstone's Commentaries they would have known that the reference to the "laws of nature" was more than "political rhetoric." Blackstone said that man must in all points conform to his maker's will. He added:

THIS will of his maker is called the law of nature....This law of nature which, being coeval with mankind and dictated by God Himself, is, of course, superior in obligation to any other. It is binding over all the globe, in all countries, and at all times. No human laws are of any validity, if contrary to this.[8]

McClellan discusses the views of Aristotle, Cicero and Locke on natural law and rights (while ignoring Blackstone in this context).

Then he questions whether Thomas Jefferson really understood what he wrote in the Declaration. McClellan wrote:

> *Like most Americans of his day, Jefferson failed to grasp the inherent contradictions between natural law and natural rights doctrines....It would be the task of later generations to sort out the confusing and sometimes conflicting precedents that had laid the foundation of rights in America. (pg.129)*

McClellan's apparent disregard and disdain for the Declaration's primary thesis—that God gave man his rights appears in his next sentence. He wrote:

> *There can be no doubt, however, that some Americans <u>thought</u> they had been endowed by their Creator with so-called natural rights and acted upon that assumption. (pg. 129) (The underlined emphasis was McClellan's.)*

The next chapter of this book shows that people at the time of the founding did believe that they had been endowed by God with their rights. They believed it because they could support that teaching in the Bible. McClellan, a constitutional conservative, continues his disparagement of the concept that the *Declaration of Independence* is America's founding document. He writes:

> *The Preamble of the Declaration of Independence, it would seem, embodies a theory of government that does not withstand the test of modern analysis. There is no denying that it contains sweeping propositions of doubtful validity. (pg. 131)*

Barnett is a libertarian and McClellan (now deceased) was a conservative. Alan Dershowitz is an ACLU-type liberal Harvard professor. He says that his book, *America Declares Independence*,[9] published in 2003...

> *...seeks to reclaim the Declaration for all Americans—indeed for all people who love liberty and abhor tyranny both of the body and the mind (page 3).*

Christopher Flannery reviewed the book in the Fall 2003 Claremont Institute *Review of Books*. He says that Dershowitz's real goal appears to be the reclaiming of the Declaration from those of the Christian Right and their view that America is a Christian nation. Dershowitz devotes about one-third of his book to fiery sermons trying to achieve that goal. His attacks are not limited to half a dozen leaders of the Christian "right" he names. Dershowitz also includes Connecticut Senator Joseph Lieberman (D), an orthodox Jew, among those he ridicules. Lieberman advocates that there is a Bible basis for the Declaration's statement that all men are endowed by their Creator with certain inalienable rights. Christopher Flannery in his review adds:

> *But ultimately—and Dershowitz is not shy about saying so—he would also reclaim the Declaration from Thomas Jefferson, himself, and from the revolutionaries of 1776.*

To do so, Dershowitz tells the reader on every fourth or fifth page that words have "different meanings" for different people in different times and places. He says:

> *As I will try to show, the very meanings of words and concepts change markedly with the times....Even words as apparently timeless as "God," "nature," "equal," and "rights" convey somewhat different meanings today than they did in 1776 (pg. 4).*

In other words, Dershowitz, like McClellan, questions whether Jefferson really understood what he wrote in the Declaration. Dershowitz questions whether the words Jefferson used mean the same thing today. This is the post-modern type of "new-think" which young college students have been fed for the last forty years.

Dershowitz's particular targets are the distinctive words of the Declaration's second paragraph. These are the words which set forth the self-evident truth that men are created equal, that they are endowed by their Creator with certain inalienable rights. Dershowitz says that concept is "nonsense on stilts (pg. 102)." Dershowitz "proves" his point saying...

> *...The American school of legal realism—beginning with [Oliver Wendell] Holmes and reaching its zenith in the mid-20th Century—changed all that. "Rights" and "equality" are purely "human inventions," "legal or moral fictions."*

In his review Flannery summarizes Dershowitz's point that Holmes efforts have been so successful that...

> *...with few exceptions today, everyone believes that morality and even truth are ever changing....evolving with experience and the views of the age.*

This is the virtually unquestioned orthodoxy of American law schools today. As a result, practically every first year law student is taught to read the Declaration and Constitution as "a text whose meaning must differ from generation to generation with changing experience."

As a result, God and the words of the Declaration have almost vanished in today's academia. Therefore, Dershowitz must find a new foundation for a "higher morality." For those, like Dershowitz, who do not believe in God, natural law, Creator-endued natural rights, unchanging truth, and absolutes of right and wrong, what is the basis of their "higher morality?" Dershowitz has an answer:

> *It is Human experience! Trial and error!...we recognize our past mistakes and try to build a better system or morality to avoid repetition of those mistakes (pg. 115)!*

For Dershowitz, because of evolution...

> *...we can be expected to have a higher morality than the Ten Commandments, because, we have much more human experience on which to base our rules than did those who wrote the Bible....Morality evolves with experience (pg. 108).*

Darwin's theory of evolution, as Chapter V will show, has had a tremendous impact not just on biology but on law, education and culture.

Dershowitz is a recognized Harvard professor and distinguished legal expert. In his book he tells how, in classes at Harvard, he moves students from faith (God) to reason (science) as the basis for their lives (pgs. 46-48).

Such doubts are deeply embedded today in education, law and much of society.

Is it any wonder, therefore, that the Minnesota State Senator quoted earlier, could defend removal of the *Declaration of Independence* from that state's proposed education standards. Senator Kelley said:

> *The Declaration of Independence has no legal status in defining people's rights and privileges.*

A 2004 state-wide meeting of school attorneys in Missouri shows how far that lack of understanding of the role of the Declaration has spread. School attorneys were discussing what religious rights if any school teachers and students have in schools today. Mention of the *Declaration of Independence* was brushed aside as irrelevant. Some even labeled citing the existence of a God who might endow men with rights as an outmoded concept. One attorney, however, got attention when he entered the conversation saying:

> *Whether there is a God or not is not important in this situation.*

He added quickly that he firmly believed in the existence of God, but whether or not God existed had no relevance to the discussion. He explained that the *Declaration of Independence* functions as the nation's articles of incorporation. It was a contract made and agreed to by representatives of the colonies. When prodded, the attorneys agreed that, under law, once parties agree to a contract it is binding, even if today people should come to believe that there is no God. He added:

> *So, as attorneys you need to realize that whether there is a God or not, you are stuck with the Declaration of Independence. It was a contract agreed to by the representatives of the thirteen colonies and the Constitution should be interpreted in that context.*

Denying that the *Declaration of Independence* served as the articles of incorporation of the new nation would have the effect of abolishing the United States. The denial would, in effect, abolish the basis on which the nation was founded and given the name, *United States*. Some of the attorneys present were challenged by the thought and asked if the attorney could put the ideas on paper.

The relationship of the *Declaration of Independence* to the Constitution does have one important and significant defender. Supreme Court Justice Clarence Thomas is described as such in an essay in the Summer 2004, Claremont Institute *Review of Books*. Edward J. Erler, professor of political science at California State, San Bernardino, says that Thomas...

> *...is not reluctant to invoke the principles of the Declaration of Independence on appropriate occasions; and he certainly understands that <u>the Constitution operates within the moral and political universe created by the Declaration.</u>*[10] *(Emphasis added.)*

The vital relationship between the Declaration and the Constitution was also explained by President John Quincy Adams. In his *Jubilee of the Constitution,* Adams wrote:

> *The virtue which had been infused into the Constitution of the United States...was no other than...those abstract principles which had been first proclaimed in the Declaration of Independence—namely the self-evident truths of the natural and unalienable rights of man...and the sovereignty of the people, always subordinate to the rule of right and wrong, and always responsible to the Supreme Ruler of the universe for the rightful exercise of that sovereign...power. <u>This was the platform upon which the Constitution of the United States had been erected.</u>[11] (Emphasis added.)*

Thomas Jefferson gave similar support to the premise that rights come from God. He wrote:

> *Can the liberties of a nation be thought secure when we have removed their only firm basis; a conviction in the minds of the people that these liberties are the gift of God? That they are not to be violated but with His wrath? Indeed, I tremble for my country when I realize that God is just, and His justice cannot sleep forever!*[12]

Adams acknowledged that liberty is the gift of God. Jefferson wrote it into the Declaration. Fifty-six men agreed and signed the Declaration. They put their lives, their fortunes and their sacred honor on the line.

But was it so? Were the founding fathers correct? Is it a Biblical concept that rights enumerated in the Declaration come from God— or were they just nice words? About half of the signers were seminary graduates. They should have known. What God wants us to know about Himself is revealed in the Bible. So if the Creator did endow men with their rights, support for those rights should be found in the Bible. A careful search shows that not only the Declaration's life, liberty and happiness are in the Bible—but also the rights spelled out in the Constitution's Bill of Rights—as the next chapter will show.

CHAPTER III

IS THERE A BIBLICAL BASIS FOR THE DECLARATION OF INDEPENDENCE AND THE U.S. CONSTITUTION?

Every good gift and every perfect gift is from above, and cometh down from the Father of lights, with whom is no variableness, neither shadow of turning.

—James 1:17

WERE THE FOUNDING FATHERS CORRECT? Were they right when they wrote **in the** *Declaration of Independence* that our rights come from God? How can we know? All that God wants us to know about Himself is revealed in the Bible. So if the Creator did endow all individuals with their rights, support for those rights should be found in the Bible.

A careful search shows that the Declaration's life, liberty and happiness are in the Bible. The rights spelled out in the Constitution's Bill of Rights can be found there also. The familiar second paragraph of the Declaration says:

We hold these truths to be self-evident, that all men are created equal, that they are endowed by their Creator with certain unalienable rights, that among these are Life, Liberty and the pursuit of Happiness.

An individual's most important right is life. The Bible says that life comes from God. Genesis 2:7 says:

And the Lord God formed man of the dust of the ground, and breathed into his nostrils the breath of life; and man became a living soul.

So the *Declaration of Independence* is correct in saying that life came from God. Liberty also is a gift of God. II Corinthians 3:17 says:

Now the Lord is that Spirit and where the Spirit of the Lord is, there is liberty.

True liberty results from the presence of God's Spirit in our lives. When individuals see themselves in bondage to desires and sins, if they believe that God the Son, Jesus Christ, died in their place and arose, God's Holy Spirit comes into their lives. The Spirit gives those individuals the desire and ability to break the chains of lust and desire. The person then becomes free to do the will of God which is the true definition of liberty.

What about the "pursuit of happiness" with which the Declaration says God endowed man? In Ecclesiastes 3:13, God's Word says:

> And also that every man should eat and drink, and enjoy the good of all his labour, it is the gift of God.

So the concept that life, liberty and the pursuit of happiness come from God is Biblical.

But what about freedom of speech, assembly and religion? What about the freedom to keep and bear arms, etc? Are they in the Bible? They are not spelled out specifically—but the founding fathers didn't say they were. The important second paragraph *Declaration of Independence* says:

> WE *hold these truths to be* self-evident, *that all men are created equal, that they are endowed by their Creator with certain inalienable rights, that among these are...*

Life, liberty and the pursuit of happiness are spelled out in the Bible. The Bible also shows that the other rights God gives man are *self-evident.* Comparing the Bible with the Constitution's Bill of Rights shows that they are *self-evident.*

AMENDMENT I AND ITS BIBLICAL BASIS

> I. *Congress shall make no law respecting an establishment of religion, or prohibiting the free exercise thereof; of abridging the freedom of speech, or of the press, or the right of people peacefully to assemble, and to petition the Government for a redress of grievances.*

Freedom of religion, speech, press, etc. are among five "self-evident" rights. The Bible shows that they are *self-evident. In Mark 16:15-16* the Lord Jesus told His disciples:

Go ye into all the world, and preach the Gospel to every creature. He that believeth and is baptized shall be saved; but he that believeth not shall be damned.

God commanded His people to go and preach. Isn't it *self-evident* then that He would also give freedom of speech so His Great Commission could be obeyed? (Of course, His command to preach the Gospel must be obeyed even where a government denies that freedom.)

Likewise, in Hebrews 10:24-25 the Bible says:

And let us consider one another to provoke unto love and to good works; Not forsaking the <u>assembling</u> of ourselves together, as the manner of some is; but exhorting one another: and so much the more, as ye see the day [of his return] approaching.

Would God command us to do something that He did not give us the right to do? So the freedom to peacefully assemble in church and elsewhere is also a Biblical concept.

What about the 1st Amendment right to petition the Government for a redress of grievances? The Bible repeatedly invites and commands God's people to bring their petitions to Him. The Lord Jesus gave those invitations in many places and many ways. Several are:

Ask and it shall be given you (Matthew 7:7); What things soever you desire; when ye pray, believe that ye receive them, and ye shall have them (Mark 11:24); And whatsoever ye shall ask in my name, that will I do (John 14:13); Verily, verily, I say unto you, Whatsoever ye shall ask the Father in my name, he will give it you. Hitherto have ye asked nothing in my name: ask, and ye shall receive, that your joy shall be full (John 16:23-24).

The God of this universe gives us the right and privilege of petitioning Him. Isn't it *self-evident* then that He would also give us the right to petition governmental leaders? Romans 13:4 says they are to be "...ministers of God to us for good." The founding fathers recognized this *self-evident* right and wrote it into the 1st Amendment.

What about freedom of the press? Actually, there were no printing presses or newspapers when the Bible was written. But there is a *self-evident* concept which applies. Psalm 68:11 says:

*The Lord gave the word: great was the company of those that
<u>published</u> it.*

The principle is Biblical. God desires that His people distribute
information. The right to do it is *self-evident.*

What about freedom of religion? The 1st Amendment says Congress can't establish how people will worship nor interfere with their
doing so. But does God actually give men the freedom of religion—a
freedom to choose whatever religion they might want? In Joshua
24:15, God's leader Joshua told the people:

> *And if it seem evil to you to serve the Lord, choose ye this day
> whom ye will serve....but as for me and my house, we will serve
> the Lord.*

In I Kings 18:21, the prophet Elijah, speaking for God, in a similar
manner, challenged the people saying:

> *How long halt ye between two opinions? If the Lord be God, follow
> him: but if Baal, then follow him.*

So God has made us free to chose—even in the area of religion.
However, having shown us that His way is through faith in Jesus
Christ, we will answer to Him someday as to how we used the
"freedom of religion" He gives us.

The phrase *separation of church and state* is not in the Constitution. However, people and the courts take the Constitutional phrase
"establishment of religion" to mean "separation of church and state."
It is so misapplied by the Courts today. The true concept of *separation of church and state* which the Bible does teach simply forbids
the state and its leaders from involving themselves in the affairs
and rituals of the church. Severe penalties were applied by God on
political leaders who involved themselves in the "work" of the
church. For example, Uzziah was one of the great kings in the
history of Israel. He reigned for fifty-two years. But he violated God's
"separation of church and state." He went into the temple of God to
burn incense upon the altar. The temple priests cautioned him that
involving himself in the ministry of the temple was a forbidden
"trespass." In anger, he rejected their warnings. As he proceeded to
offer the incense, II Kings 26:25-26 says he was smitten by the Lord
with leprosy and he remained a leper until he died.

Uzziah was not the only king of Israel who was judged by God for violating the "separation of church and state." Saul was Israel's first king. Samuel was the prophet and priest. In I Samuel 13:8, in a time of trouble, King Saul wanted to have a sacrifice offered. As a priest, Samuel had the responsibility to offer the sacrifices. When Samuel was delayed, impatient Saul offered the sacrifice himself. In doing so, he violated the wall of separation between "church and state." Samuel returned and told King Saul:

> *Thou has done foolishly: for thou has not kept the commandment of the Lord thy God, which he commanded thee....But now thy kingdom shall not continue.*

Violating the wall of separation God established to keep the state and its rulers from intruding into God's ministry is a serious thing. Uzziah did so and lived out his life as a leper. Saul lost his kingdom. The founding fathers recognized this Biblical separation of church and state and wrote it into the Bill of Rights.

THE BIBLE AND AMENDMENT II

> *II. A well regulated Militia, being necessary to the security of a free State, the right of the people to keep and bear Arms, shall not be infringed.*

Is the freedom to keep and bear arms a *self-evident* Biblical right? Is it a right with which our Creator would endow us? In Luke 22:35-36, just before the Lord Jesus went to the Cross, He spoke with his disciples and said:

> *When I sent you without purse, and scrip, and shoes, lacked ye any thing? And they said, Nothing. Then he said unto them, But now, he that hath a purse, let him take it, and likewise his scrip: and he that hath no sword, let him sell his garment, and buy one.*

So God means for man to have a right of self defense—the right to keep and bear arms. In fact, the words of the Lord Jesus here appears to make it not just a right, but a duty. The 2nd Amendment has a Biblical basis.

THE BIBLE AND AMENDMENTS III AND IV

The 3rd and 4th Amendments prohibit the government from infringing upon or interfering with the sanctity of our homes. Those amendments are:

III. No Soldier shall in time of peace be quartered in any home, without the consent of the owner, nor in time of war, but in a manner to be prescribed by law.

IV. The right of the people to be secure in their persons, houses, papers and effects, against unreasonable searches and seizures, shall not be violated, and no Warrants shall issue, but upon probable cause, supported by Oath or affirmation, and particularly describing the place to be searched, and the persons or things to be seized.

The Biblical basis for the sanctity of an individual's home can be found in Deuteronomy 24:10-11 which says:

And when thou dost lend they brother anything, thou shalt not go into his house to fetch his pledge. Thou shalt stand abroad, and the man to whom thou dost lend shall bring out the pledge unto thee.

A pledge is made as security or collateral for a loan. If the loan is not paid, God says that the man who made the loan cannot go into the creditor's home to claim what is due. The 3rd and 4th Amendments which protect the sanctity of the home have a Biblical basis.

THE BIBLE AND AMENDMENT V

No person shall be held to answer for a capital, or otherwise infamous crime, unless on a presentment or indictment of a Grand Jury, except in cases arising in the land or naval forces, or in the Militia, when in actual service in time of War or public danger; nor shall any person be subject for the same offense to be twice put in jeopardy of life or limb, nor shall be compelled in any criminal case to be a witness against himself, nor be deprived of life, liberty or property, without due process of law; nor shall private property be taken for public use without just compensation.

To avoid writing a full book or books on the Fifth Amendment, the Biblical basis for only two sections will be presented here. The best known section of the Fifth Amendment provides that no one shall be compelled to be a witness against himself. This protects an individual from being tortured or forced in some other way to confess, which happens in much of the world. The Biblical basis for this protection against self incrimination is found in Deuteronomy 19:15 which says:

> *One witness shall not rise up against a man for any iniquity, or for any sin, in any sin that he sinneth: at the mouth of two witnesses, or at the mouth of three witnesses, shall the matter be established.*

If an individual were *compelled* to testify against himself and he confessed, there would only be one witness. That would violate the Biblical standard for determining truth.

Amendment V also provides that no individual shall be put in jeopardy a second time for the same offense. Once tried and found not guilty or tried, found guilty and punished an individual cannot be charged a second time for the same offense. There is a theological and Biblical basis for this provision. I John 2:1-2 says:

> *My little children, these things write I unto you, that ye sin not. And if any man sin, we have an advocate with the Father, Jesus Christ the righteous: And he is the propitiation [payment] for our sins: and not for ours only, but also for the sins of the whole world.*

God so loved a world of sinners that Jesus Christ came and died to pay the penalty for those who believe on Him. On that basis, those who have believed that the Lord Jesus already died in their place cannot be placed at risk of being found guilty a second time. Their sins have already been paid for by the shedding of the blood of Christ. The Lord Jesus sits at the right hand of the Father as our "advocate." He is, in effect, our lawyer. When we sin, after we have believed that He died for all of our personal sins, He tells the Father that the Blood He shed was the payment for those sins. Therefore, there can be no double jeopardy. For those people, in John 5:24, the Lord Jesus promises:

> *Verily, verily, I say unto you. He that heareth my word, and believeth on him that sent me, hath everlasting life, and shall not come into condemnation; but is passed from death unto life.*

Those who trust that Christ answered for them and died in their place will never have to answer a second time for their sins. They are free! It is on this basis that the Fifth Amendment prohibits trying an individual a second time for any crime. To do so would be double jeopardy.

THE BIBLE AND AMENDMENTS VI AND VII

Denial of the right to trial by jury was a key reason cited in the *Declaration of Independence* for breaking with England. That right was written into the Bill of Rights.

> *VI. In all criminal prosecutions, the accused shall enjoy the right to a speedy trial, by an impartial jury of the State and district wherein the crime shall have been committed; which district shall have been previously ascertained by law, and to be informed of the nature and cause of the accusation; to be confronted with the witnesses against him; to have compulsory process for obtaining witnesses in his favor, and to have assistance of counsel for his defense.*

> *VII. In suits at common law, where the value in controversy shall exceed twenty dollars, the right of trial by jury shall be preserved, and no fact tried by jury shall be otherwise re-examined in any Court of the United States, than according to the rules of common law.*

The right for trial by a jury of our peers has a Biblical basis. I Corinthians 6:2-3 provides that saints (fellow Christians), and not some ecclesiastical authority should judge disputes in the church and in society. It says:

> *Do ye not know that the saints shall judge the world? and if the world shall be judged by you, are ye not worthy to judge the smallest matters? Know ye not that we shall judge angels? how much more things that pertain to this life?*

In Matthew 18:15-19, the Lord Jesus spelled out the way differences should be resolved. The final authority when Christians disagree is not some ecclesiastical authority but the body of believers in the church, functioning, in effect, as a jury.

THE BIBLE AND AMENDMENT EIGHT

> *VIII. Excessive bail shall not be required, nor excessive fines imposed, nor cruel and unusual punishments inflicted.*

The Biblical basis for limiting cruel and excessive punishments is found in Deuteronomy 25:2-3 which says:

> *And it shall be, if the wicked man be worthy to be beaten, that the judge shall cause him to lie down, and to be beaten before his face, according to his fault, by a certain number. Forty stripes he may*

give him, and not exceed: lest, if he should exceed, and beat him above these with many stripes, then thy brother should seem vile unto thee.

THE BIBLE AND AMENDMENTS IX AND X

The Federal Government has usurped powers over the operations of the states and the lives of the people. It has been done in ways the founders could never have envisioned. The runaway power of the federal government could be curbed IF the states and the people were to understand and enforce the Ninth and Tenth Amendments to the Constitution. Those amendments say:

IX. The enumeration in the Constitution of certain rights shall not be construed to deny or disparage others retained by the people.

X. The powers not delegated to the United States by the Constitution, nor prohibited by it to the States, are reserved to the States respectively, or to the people.

The Ninth and Tenth Amendments are largely ignored today. Do these amendments have a Biblical basis? The phrase in the *Declaration of Independence* which states that the government was to be formed "with the consent of the governed" is the key. It should be obvious then that the federal government would only have the rights the people through their States would agree to give it. All other rights would be retained by the people and those they gave to the States when they wrote their State constitutions.

Those *legal* arguments supporting the Ninth and Tenth Amendments are based on the Declaration's "the consent of the governed" phrase.

THE BIBLE AND CONSENT OF THE GOVERNED

The Declaration says "That to secure these [God-given] Rights, Governments are instituted among Men, deriving their just Powers from the Consent of the Governed...." That was the authority for forming a government by writing the Constitution. It has a Biblical basis. In Daniel 4:28-37, the Bible sets forth the truth that it is God who sets up governments and takes them down. That could cause some to raise a question about whether there is Biblical support for the Declaration's concept that governments should be formed with "the consent of the governed."

The "consent of the governed" is illustrated in the Bible. In I Samuel 16 God sent his prophet Samuel to anoint David as Israel's king. Samuel anointed David (who was about fifteen years old at the time). It happened about one year before young David defeated Goliath. Saul, the king David was to replace, wasn't anxious to be replaced. Even though David had been chosen by God and anointed as king, he didn't get to rule immediately.

Fifteen years passed. Then in II Samuel 5:1-3, all the tribes of Israel came to David and the scripture says:

So all the elders of Israel came to the king to Hebron; David made a league with them in Hebron before the Lord; and they anointed David king over Israel. David was thirty years old when he began to reign, and he reigned for forty years.

Although David had been named king by God, it was fifteen years before he received the "consent of the governed." Only then could David start ruling as king.

So even the *"consent of the governed"* provision of the Declaration has a clear cut Biblical basis. The founding fathers as Biblical scholars saw and fit these things together. At the time, no governments except for Israel had ever had "the consent of the governed."

THE DECLARATION IS FOR ALL PEOPLE

The *Declaration of Independence* is America's foundational document. The Constitution was written to implement the concept that men are endowed by their Creator with certain rights AND that governments are instituted among men to secure these rights. When understood, that truth can revolutionize American society and its laws. That truth can even revolutionize the world.

The *Declaration of Independence* is usually regarded as an *American* document—and it is. However, if the concept that man's rights come from God is true—and it is—*then all men everywhere are born with the same God-given rights Americans enjoy.* The *Declaration of Independence* proclaims God's truth and it applies to all men because *God is no respecter of persons.*

God endows everyone born into the world with the same basic rights every American enjoys and often takes for granted. Why then, have so few people, ever lived in real freedom?

Men can only enjoy and exercise their God-given rights to the extent that the nation in which they live is "a nation under God." Freedom-seeking people around the world need to hear this message. It has power no man-made message possesses.

Some years ago, the author of this book had an opportunity to outline this truth to a meeting of 1,500 preachers. They were from India, South Africa, Pakistan, Indonesia, Central and South America, South Korea, free China, and half a dozen struggling African states. They had been guests in America for two weeks. They had seen and tasted of the unbelievable (for them) blessings and material prosperity Americans enjoy. In the message they heard the truth that Americans enjoyed their tremendous blessings, their rights and their freedom not because Americans were smarter or worked harder or had a better Constitution than others in the world. Americans have the blessings these foreign guests had been observing because America had been founded as "a nation under God." America enjoys its blessings because of God's Word which promises:

Blessed is the nation whose God is the Lord; and the people whom he hath chosen for his own inheritance. (Psalm 33:12)

The 1500 preachers from all over the world heard the basis upon which America was established. They caught the vision that they too had been endowed by their Creator with the same rights and freedoms Americans had. They exploded with excitement. Many dedicated themselves to returning home to work to make their countries "nations under God" also.

All over the world people are seeking freedom. These freedom seekers must be given a vision for what made America great. It is the message that God has endowed all men with certain unalienable rights. Those rights can only be exercised and enjoyed *in a nation whose God is the Lord.*

THE CHALLENGE FOR AMERICANS

The message has power. Before Americans and their missionaries can take it to the world, it must be relearned in the United States.

The 4th of July each year would be an appropriate time for Americans to dedicate themselves to the task of restoring the real message of the *Declaration of Independence*. It must be restored in our hearts, our homes, our schools, our churches and our government. Once that dedication is made, then the message should be raised daily throughout the year.

It would also be appropriate to evaluate how far America has moved from being truly "One Nation Under God." We, like all of the world's people, have been given our rights by God. But we can only continue to enjoy them as long as we are truly "One Nation Under God." The process starts when individuals whose own lives are "Under God" challenge others, their churches, the schools, and ultimately the courts to return America to its foundations.

You can help by starting to ask everyone you meet, in as many ways as possible, this big question:

How can "rights" be found to abort babies, engage in sodomy or form same sex unions in a Constitution written to make secure the rights which the Declaration of Independence says God gives us?

CHAPTER IV

CAN HISTORY PROVE THAT THE UNITED STATES WAS FOUNDED AS A NATION UNDER GOD?

...this is a Christian nation....This is historically true. From the discovery of this continent to the present hour, there is a single voice making this affirmation....These are not individual sayings, declarations of private persons: they are organic utterances: they speak the voice of the entire people....These and many other matters ...add a volume of unofficial declarations to the mass of organic utterances that this is a Christian nation.[1]
Church of the Holy Trinity v. U.S.
—U.S. Supreme Court, 1892

IS IT REALLY TRUE that America was founded as a nation under God? Was the Declaration correct when it said that the rights Americans enjoy come from God? Was the U.S. Supreme Court correct in 1892 when it declared, "This is a Christian nation."

The first "proof" or evidence that America was founded as a nation under God is the nation's founding document the *Declaration of Independence*. Its key phrase proclaims that God is the source of man's inherent rights. Secondly, the Founding Fathers repeatedly stated their belief that acceptance of God and His Word was the only sure foundation for the nation and its freedom. Finally, the Bible itself shows that the United States was founded "as a nation under God."

Psalm 33:12 says, "Blessed is the nation whose God is the Lord." The United States has been blessed in every way as no other nation in history has been. That indicates, as Psalm 33:12 says, that the nation so abundantly blessed was indeed founded "under God."

Congress reaffirmed the founding fact in 1954. It added "One nation under God" to the Pledge of Allegiance.

Shortly after the change was made a preacher at a meeting in Washington, D.C. observed, "Isn't it interesting that when we were truly a nation under God, we didn't feel the need to say so." Cultural changes he was seeing then prompted his comment. It would be a few years before the Supreme Court banned prayer and Bible reading in the schools. In the years that followed, ongoing Court "discoveries" made abortion and the practice of sodomy and distribution of pornography constitutional. But that preacher was already seeing changes.

What produced the changes? To understand the transformation of America's courts, legal system and culture, it is necessary to study the foundations from which the American courts, legal system, culture and way of life grew. Such a study is essential if the culture and way of life on which America grew great is ever to be restored.

The foundation for the entire *Declaration of Independence* and its claim that the colonies had a right to separate from England is found in the first paragraph of the Declaration. Although it is foundational, that first paragraph is less quoted and less understood than the second paragraph. The second paragraph sets forth the better known truth that "we were endowed by our Creator with certain inalienable rights." The important first paragraph says:

> *WHEN in the Course of human Events, it becomes necessary for one People to dissolve the Political Bands which have connected them with another, and to assume among the Powers of the Earth, the separate and equal Station to which the Laws of Nature and of Nature's God entitle them, a decent Respect to the Opinions of Mankind requires that they should declare the causes which impel them to the Separation.*

Understanding of the term *The Laws of Nature and of Nature's God* has been eroded, lost or ignored in the last 225 years. The phrase is more than just a few nice words. *The Laws of Nature and Nature's God* had important historical, judicial, theological and political meaning for centuries in England. The phrase was widely known and understood in the colonies at the time of the founding. Understanding *The Laws of Nature and Nature's God* is the key to understanding the system of law and justice at the time of the nation's founding. It is also the key to understanding how it has gone astray since.

The first edition of the *Encyclopedia Britannica* was published in 1771. That was five years before the *Declaration of Independence* was written. It said of the law of nature:

The Law of Nature is that which God has prescribed to all men, by the internal dictate of reason....It is discovered by a just consideration of the agreeableness or disagreeableness of human actions to the nature of man.

The Encyclopedia adds that the law of nature...

...comprehends all the duties we owe either to the Supreme Being; to ourselves; or to our neighbour—such as reverence to God; self defense; temperance; honour to our parents; benevolence to all; a strict adherence to our engagements; gratitude, &c.

In other words, the law of nature was just that which every decent person would agree should be the basis for society. At the time, because it was accepted that it came from God, the Encyclopedia stated:

The Law of Nature, where it either commands or forbids, is immutable and cannot be controlled by any human author.

Where did *The Laws of Nature* come from? The sixth president of the United States, John Quincy Adams, said that the laws of nature...

...presupposes the existence of a God, the moral ruler of the universe, and a rule of right and wrong, of just and unjust, binding upon man, preceding all institutions of human society and government.[2]

Adams statement is similar to those of many others down through history. No matter how primitive, in every society there have always been certain accepted rules of conduct and morality. They were frequently described as the *laws of nature*. How did such *laws of nature* develop even in societies which never had the Bible? The Bible has the answer. In Romans 2:14-15, God's Word contrasts those, unlike Israel, who did not get God's law by revelation. It says:

For when the Gentiles, which have not the law, do by nature the things contained in the law, these, having not the law, are a law unto themselves: Which shew the work of the law written in their hearts, their conscience also bearing witness, and their thoughts the mean while accusing or else excusing one another.

The founders and others down through history, going back even to Aristotle and Plato recognized this truth. They observed, as this Scripture explains, that men have within themselves concepts of right and wrong, respect for life, respect for property, etc. This internal sense of morality was frequently regarded or called *natural law* and it came to have actual legal standing.

Alexander Hamilton, a signer of the Constitution and George Washington's Treasury Secretary, wrote:

> The law of nature, "which, being coeval with mankind and dictated by God Himself, is, of course, superior in obligation to any other. It is binding over all the globe, in all countries, and at all times. No human laws are of any validity, if contrary to this."[3]

Alexander Hamilton was directly quoting Sir William Blackstone's *Commentaries on the Laws of England*. The founders were familiar with Blackstone. It was on this basis and understanding that the *Declaration of Independence* was written and the Constitution adopted. Their purpose was to make secure the rights God bestowed upon man.

The concept of laws of nature, which came to be regarded as *natural law*, was widely known from the writings of Sir William Blackstone. Almost from the time of the nation's founding Blackstone's *Commentaries on the Law of England* was the textbook of every student of law in the colonies and the nation they formed. Blackstone remained such until the early 1900s. Blackstone's work even got widespread reading among the general public.

Blackstone's Commentaries basically codified English common law. Common law was what courts and judges in England applied and enforced for hundreds of years. Common law, an important legal term, is:

> The body of customary law, based upon judicial decisions and embodied in reports of decided cases, which originated in England in the early Middle Ages in the decisions of local courts that applied custom and reason to everyday disputes.[4]

Common law, on which Blackstone based his Commentaries, grew over the centuries. It came largely from natural law and divine revelation in the Holy Scriptures. Blackstone's compilation of the common law emphasized God-given rights and liberties. Although it was not his intention, his teaching on "the laws of nature and nature's God" inspired the basis the founding fathers gave in the *Declaration of Independence* for separating from England. Blackstone in his Commentaries contended, taught and showed that...

> UPON *two foundations, the law of nature and the law of revelation [the Bible], depend all human laws; that is to say, no human laws should be suffered to contradict these.*[5]

Blackstone was drawing upon centuries of English legal history. In the early 1500s, a three-tier hierarchy of law was recognized as the basis for what was regarded as *common law*. It started with the law of God as revealed in the Bible. Natural law (developed through reason and experience) followed. Finally, human or positive law was made by governmental authorities. None of it could conflict with the law of God. Based on that hierarchy of law, in the early 1600s, the brilliant and principled English jurist Sir Edward Coke established the principle...

> ...*when an Act of Parliament (or the King) is against common right or reason or repugnant or impossible to be performed, the common law will control it, and adjudge such act to be void.*[6]

That set the standard. Judges are seen to have the authority, if rightly used, to overrule actions of the legislature or the executive.

The founders accepted Blackstone's teaching. They often amplified upon it. The first chief justice of the U.S. Supreme Court, John Jay, spelled out the source of *natural law*. He wrote:

> *The moral, or natural law, was given by the sovereign of the universe to all mankind.*[7]

James Wilson was one of only six men who signed both the *Declaration of Independence* and the U.S. Constitution. He was appointed to the first U.S. Supreme Court by George Washington. The American view of natural law at the time of the founding of the United States was not a secular one. Of natural law Wilson wrote:

> *As promulgated by reason and the moral sense. it has been called natural; as promulgated by the Holy Scriptures, it has been called revealed law. As addressed to men, it has been denominated the law of nature; as addressed to political societies, it has been denominated the law of nations. But it should always be remembered that this law, natural or revealed, made for men or for*

nations, flows from the same divine source; it is the law of God....Human law must rest its authority ultimately upon the authority of that law which is divine.[8]

Natural law was based upon reason and experience as to what was regarded as right or natural. Wilson, Blackstone and others used the term *revealed law* to mean that which comes from God through the Holy Scriptures. These concepts of the basis of law and government were widely held at the time of the founding of the nation. Almost half of those who signed the *Declaration of Independence* were seminary graduates. Many were students of John Witherspoon, who was himself a signer. Witherspoon was both a preacher and president of Princeton College. Among his students were:

A President, Vice President, three Supreme Court Justices, ten Cabinet members, twelve Governors, twenty-one Senators, thirty-nine Representatives in Congress, as well as numerous delegates to the Continental Congress and the Constitutional Convention. One of his students was James Madison who served eight years as Secretary of State and eight years as President of the United States. Madison, known by many as the "Chief Architect of the Constitution" was the original author of the Bill of Rights.[9]

On the future of America, Madison wrote:

We have staked the whole future of American civilization, not upon the power of government, far from it. We have staked the future of all of our political institutions upon the capacity of mankind for self-government; upon the capacity of each and all of us to government ourselves, to control ourselves, to sustain ourselves according to the Ten Commandments of God.[10]

Madison was not alone. George Washington said:

Of all dispositions and habits which lead to political prosperity. Religion and morality are indispensable supports.[11]

The second president, John Adams, said:

Our Constitution was made only for a moral and religious people. It is wholly inadequate to the government of any other.[12]

There are many religions. Were these founders of the United States speaking of religion, in general, or were they basing their hopes on a specific religion? President Adams answered that ques-

tion. In a letter to Thomas Jefferson on December 25, 1813 Adams
wrote:

> *I have examined all religions, as well as my narrow sphere, my
> straightened means, and my busy life would allow; and the result
> is that the Bible is the best Book in the world.*[13]

Patrick Henry made it even clearer. He wrote:

> *It cannot be emphasized too strongly or too often that this great
> nation was founded, not by religionists, but by Christians; not on
> religions, but on the Gospel of Jesus Christ.*[14]

It was to protect the right to practice Christianity that the 1st
Amendment to the Constitution was adopted. Mis-applied today,
the 1st Amendment is being used to almost ban the public acknowledgement of God.

Joseph Story was the youngest man ever appointed to the U.S.
Supreme Court. He was appointed at age 34 by President James
Madison. Story served 34 years before he died in 1845. His com-
ments on the 1st Amendment give real insight into its original
intent. In his 1840 *A Familiar Exposition of the Constitution of the
United States,* Story wrote:

> *We are not to attribute this prohibition of a national religious
> establishment [in the First Amendment] to an indifference to
> religion in general. and especially to Christianity (which none
> could hold in more reverence than the framers of the Constitu-
> tion)....*

> *Probably, at the time of the adoption of the Constitution, and of
> the Amendment to it now under consideration, the general, if not
> the universal, sentiment in America was, that Christianity ought
> to receive encouragement from the State so far as was not incom-
> patible with the private rights of conscience and freedom of
> religious worship.*

> *Any attempt to level all religions, and to make it a matter of state
> policy to hold all in utter indifference, would have created univer-
> sal disapprobation, if not universal indignation.*[15]

In his commentary on the 1st Amendment's original meaning,
Justice Story wrote:

> *The real object of the First Amendment was not to countenance,
> much less advance Mohammedanism, or Judaism, or infidelity,*

by prostrating Christianity, but to exclude all rivalry among Christian sects [denominations] and to prevent any national ecclesiastical patronage of the national government.[16]

Many early lawyers, like so many signers of the *Declaration of Independence* were seminary graduates. Many others who became lawyers were trained by "reading law." In effect, they served apprenticeships. They learned the "trade" by working under lawyers while studying Blackstone and court decisions. In the process they were constantly being exposed to scripture as the basis for law.

For example, Charles Graddison Finney wanted to be a lawyer. As the custom was in those days, he went to work in a law office. Finney was not a Christian in a Bible sense. However, as he studied Blackstone and court decisions he found the Bible referenced continually. Finney decided that if he were to be a successful lawyer he needed to know more about the Word of God. As he studied the Bible Finney came to see and believe that he was one of the sinners for whom Jesus died. He was saved. He soon left the study of law to preach the Gospel. Finney became the most powerful evangelist of the first half of the 19th Century.

That story isn't repeated often today in the formal training of lawyers. As a result, the nation has been moved from where it was founded as "One Nation Under God."

CHAPTER V

TWO ACADEMIC THEORIES CHANGED
AMERICA'S LAW AND CULTURE

Beware lest any man spoil you through philosophy and vain deceit, after the tradition of men, after the rudiments of the world, and not after Christ.
—Colossians 2:8

THE LAWS OF NATURE AND NATURE'S GOD on which the *Declaration of Independence,* the U.S. Constitution and the common law foundations of the American justice system were Biblical. The courts largely stayed with those traditions and the concepts of *absolutes* through much of the 19th Century. Abortion, sodomy, and immorality were illegal. Marriage, home and family were supported in law. Prayer, Bible reading and the posting of the Ten Commandments in school were permitted or required.

Two theories or philosophies developed in the 1800s which in time dramatically impacted law, justice, education, science and many churches. This didn't happen overnight. The two men responsible were Georg Wilhelm Hegel, a German philosopher, and Charles Darwin, the Englishman who popularized the theory of evolution. Their theories revolutionized the entire culture, not just the fields in which they worked. Hegel and Darwin "worked" in different areas. The work of both, however, rested on the theory that there are no absolutes because all things are changing continually. All things are constantly evolving.

Georg Wilhelm Hegel, a German, became one of the most prominent and influential philosophers of the 19th Century. He developed a system for applying *dialectics* to almost everything in society.[1]

The Dictionary of Philosophical Terms and Names[2] described *dialectics* as...

> *...the process of thinking by means of dialogue, discussion or argument.*

Dialectics, going back to the ancient Greek philosophers (Plato, Socrates, Aristotle, etc.), glorifies human reason. Dialectics places reason above facts and revelation in seeking truth. Therefore, dialectics is a way for...

> ...*moving people (or philosophers, teachers, pastors, lawyers, judges. etc.) away from absolute truth or values toward a group consensus in order to accomplish "group goals."*

Summed up, *reasoning* seeks reconciliation of the conflict which develops between facts and absolutes (*thou shall* or *thou shall not*) and feelings (*it could be* or *it ought to be*). For Hegel, there were no absolutes. Everything in nature, life and law were in a state of constant change.

Richard Paul, an influential socio-psychologist, in his book, *Critical Thinking: What Every Person Needs To Survive In A Rapidly Changing World,* put his finger on the *reasoning* which is at the heart of dialectics. He said:

> *We must come to define ourselves...as people who reason their way into, and can be reasoned out of, beliefs.*[3]

How did Hegel's dialectics or rules of reasoning move people from being self-governing, God-fearing individuals to being members of a pragmatic, consensus-controlled group? The MSN Encarta Encyclopedia summarized Hegel's contribution this way:

> *The dialectical method involves the notion that all movement, or process, or progress [change], is the result of the conflict of opposites. Traditionally, this dimension of Hegel's thought has been analyzed in terms of the categories of thesis, antithesis, and synthesis. Although Hegel tended to avoid these terms, they are helpful in understanding his concept of the dialectic.*[4]

A simplified, down-to-earth illustration or explanation of how the dialectic works in a group is:

> *THESIS is what you believe is true for yourself.*

> *ANTITHESIS is what others believe is true for themselves [any differences produce conflict].*

> *SYNTHESIS is the consensus which develops out of conflict as you and others, through reasoning, come to agree on what should be generally true for everyone.*

The concept can be illustrated this way:

THESIS can represent your original position or fact on any issue such as—"The Bible says it is wrong to lie."

ANTITHESIS is a different position within the group on the same issue based on feelings: "It is all right to lie to get out of a bad situation—or to avoid hurting another."

SYNTHESIS is the compromise, the finding of unity to resolve the issue and rationally justify behavior: "It is O.K. to lie providing it is justifiable in light of the situation, is beneficial to others, and doesn't hurt anybody."

For Hegel, morality starts as *individual conscience*—the *thesis*. Differing views produce the *antithesis*. The conflict between the *thesis* and the *antithesis* results in *synthesis* which is social ethics. For Hegel *social ethics* is not the product of individual judgment but rather a "consensus" developed within the group. For Hegel, individuals can only be complete as part of the *group*. The on-line *MSN Encyclopedia* summarized Hegel's position this way:

Hegel considered membership in the state one of the individual's highest duties. Ideally, the state is the manifestation of the general will, which is the highest expression of the ethical spirit. Obedience to the general will is the act of a free and rational individual.[5]

In other words, to be "a free and rational individual" it is necessary to put aside your own views and beliefs and submit to the *consensus* of the group. In effect, this means that the individual has value and reality only as a part of a greater and unified whole.

The *Grolier Encyclopedia* sees Hegel as saying that true freedom...

...is achieved only as the partial and incomplete desires of the individual are overcome and integrated into the unified system of the state in which the will of one is replaced by the will of all.[6]

This view permeates totalitarian governments. It is in complete conflict with the precepts of the *common law*. Biblical common law traditions emphasized the freedom and liberty of the individual and his property. Hegel's *social ethics* view has achieved deep roots and influence in education, politics, the media and too many churches.

Application of Hegel's dialectic became a key basis for what by the turn of the 20th Century came to be known in law as *sociological jurisprudence.*[7] This is the process through which the courts and law moved away from the absolutes of seeing and applying the law as "it is written." Instead court decisions are based on "it ought to be" or "it could be." *Sociological jurisprudence* places the "needs of the group" over the long-held common law protections of the individual's right to his life and his property. Such a Hegelian *synthesis* is impossible for those who continue trusting and obeying God.

The other far-reaching 19th Century academic development was widespread acceptance of Charles Darwin's theory of biological evolution. Set forth in his 1859 book, *The Origin of the Species,*[8] Darwin's theories had a relationship to those of Hegel. Whereas, Hegel saw all truth in a constant state of change, Darwin saw similar changes in nature through evolution.

John Whitehead's book *The Second American Revolution* quotes Julian Huxley, the English humanist. Huxley noted that Darwin's theory of biological evolution grew to encompassing such disciplines as...

> ...*law and religion...until we are enabled to see evolution as a universal, all pervading process.*[9]

The *Encyclopedia Britannica* quoted Huxley who wrote:

> *There proceeded during the 19th Century, under the influence of the evolutionary concept, a thorough going transformation of older studies like History, Law, and Political Economy; and the creation of new ones like Anthropology, Social Psychology, Comparative Religion, Criminology, Social Geography.*[10]

Hegel's dialectic concepts and Darwinian evolution influenced key law school professors. Christopher Columbus Langdell became dean of the Harvard Law School in the 1870s. He had been deeply influenced by Charles Darwin and his evolutionary theories. Of course, by that time, anyone whose thinking and beliefs were not solidly based on the absolutes of the common law and God's Word was also susceptible to Hegel's teaching. If everything is constantly changing, Langdell found a basis for theorizing that law should also be evolving.

At Harvard, Langdell introduced the concept of using *Case Law* as the basis for making judicial decisions. What a judge decided in a case became law and was to be applied as the newly "evolved" law in future cases.[11] Under Blackstone, a decision in an earlier court case applied only to that case. It was not *law* but could be considered as *evidence* of what the law was.

From the time of the founding of America until the end of the Civil War, the common law and Blackstone's Commentaries on it were the basic standards on which lawyers were trained. It was on this basis that judges made their decisions. The role of the judge during that time was to read and analyze the *established law*. Having done so, the judge then applied what had been written in making his decision. Blackstone had taught how to do it. In his Commentaries, he laid out the method for interpreting laws (or the Constitution which was to come). He wrote:

> *The fairest and most rational method to interpret the will of the legislator, is by exploring his intentions at the time when the law was made, by signs the most natural and probable. And these signs are either the words, the context, the subject matter, the effects and consequence, or the spirit and reason of the law.*[12]

With the switch to Langdell's *case law* approach, a judge's decision became the new law. It would be accepted as law and applied as a precedent in other courts unless it had been reversed by a higher court. This laid the foundation on which activist judges could start remaking the law, the courts and the legal system. As judges (including those on the Supreme Court) handed down decisions, the decisions became the new law. The change didn't happen dramatically overnight, but the foundation was being laid. The largely Biblically-based absolutes of the common law and the Constitution would evolve into a new legal concept called *sociological jurisprudence*. Rather than applying established law, judges could make decisions based on the needs of society as determined by psychologists, sociologists, economists, and organized pressure groups. Within 100 years, the U.S. Supreme Court, using the principles of *sociological jurisprudence* found or invented "rights" in the U.S. Constitution which have turned the justice system and the culture upside down.

James Barr Ames was a Langdell student at Harvard. He followed Langdell as Dean of the Law School. *The Columbia Encyclopedia, Sixth Edition, 2001* said that Ames insisted...

> *...that legal education should require the study of actual cases instead of abstract principles of law. He was instrumental in introducing the case method in the teaching of law, a method in general use by American law schools at the time of his death.*[13]

The change from teaching what Ames called "abstract principles of law" to the case law approach explains what has happened in America's courts. This is why only two out of 100 lawyers and judges reported in the survey quoted earlier reported that they ever read and studied the U.S. Constitution in constitutional law classes.

Ames downplayed the "abstract principles of law." Learning such principles challenges those studying law to think about why and how the principles developed and the foundations (often scriptural) on which law was based.

Without a study of abstract but absolute principles, the Constitution, law and other disciplines degenerate into the state described in the closing verse of the Old Testament book of Judges. Judges recorded an awful period of violence, brutality and bloodshed. The book concluded with the statement that explained the turmoil. It said that it was a period when there was no ultimate authority in Israel and...

> *...every man did that which was right in his own eyes (Judges 21:25b).*

Man becomes the ultimate authority in what is called *Secular Humanism*. This is the controlling philosophy in most of education and in the social sciences. *Secular Humanism* is the philosophy which underlies *sociological jurisprudence*.

CHAPTER VI

HOW SOCIOLOGICAL JURISPRUDENCE HAS CHANGED THE LAW AND CULTURE

*We are back to the state as the unchallengeable authority be-
hind legal precepts. The state takes the place of Jehovah
handing the tablets of the law to Moses.[1]*
                                        —Roscoe Pound, Dean,
                                        Harvard Law School, 1924

ROSCOE POUND WAS A STUDENT of Langdell and Ames at
Harvard. He learned his lessons well. Pound never earned his law
degree at Harvard, but he was admitted to the bar. From 1916 to
1936 he was the influential dean of Harvard Law School.

He was described by the *Encyclopedia Britannica* as the eminent
pioneer and champion of modern *sociological jurisprudence* in the
United States. One account of his life asked:

> *How did this child, born in Lincoln, Nebraska on the Western
> Frontier of the United States in 1870, change not only the teaching
> of the Law in law schools but the interpretation of the law itself
> by practicing lawyers and judges...? Pound saw the necessity for
> the law to change to face the challenge of the profound sociological
> changes of the twentieth century. His ideas were foundational to
> much of the New Deal legislation sponsored by President
> Franklin D. Roosevelt. Pound was the chief advocate in the United
> States of adjusting the law to social conditions.[2]*

Nine years before he became head of Harvard Law School Pound
spelled out his views for turning America's Bible-based legal system
upside down. In two presentations to the American Bar Association
Pound spoke on "The Need for a Sociological Jurisprudence."[3]
Pound proposed alternatives to the abstract philosophy and principles on which the age-old common law was built. He said that
teachers...

...while teaching the actual law by which courts decide, should give their teaching the color which will fit new generations of lawyers to lead the people as they should....To this end it is the duty of teachers of law, while they teach scrupulously the law that the courts administer, to teach it in the spirit and from the standpoint of the political, economic and sociological learning of today. It is their task to create in this country true sociological jurisprudence.

Sociological jurisprudence advocated that laws should be changed to satisfy what experts (social scientists) theorized were the needs and wants of society. Judges would substitute the teachings of sociologists, psychologists and other social scientists for the traditional common law emphasis on protecting the freedom of the individual and his property. This was to be done partially through legislation but more through *judge-made law*.

In his writings, Pound admitted that only through guile and deceit could judge-made laws be used to transform America's legal system. Replacing the common law justice system handed down from the time of America's founding was his goal.

Basically, the law would be changed through the case law approach developed at Harvard by C.C. Langdell, as was explained in the previous chapter. Oliver Wendell Holmes, Jr., known as the Great Dissenter, Louis Brandeis, a student of Langdell at Harvard, and Benjamin Cardozo were Supreme Court justices. They used their positions on the nation's highest court to promote Pound's sociological jurisprudence approach to changing the law.[4]

By the end of the 20th Century and the start of the 21st, eighty years of sociological jurisprudence had transformed America's law, culture, marriage and families. To understand how the sociological jurisprudence goals were accomplished, one must study Roscoe Pound, his life and his writings. Pound's impact on America's courts, justice system and culture continues even today. It is carried on by thousands of future lawyers, judges, law school professors and political office holders. Pound had a part in training them at Harvard.

After studying law under Langdell and James Barr Ames at Harvard, Pound studied botany. Earning a Ph.D. in botany at the

University of Nebraska grounded Pound in Darwin's theories of biological evolution.

By the time Pound became dean of the Harvard law school, he was also enthralled with the philosophy of the mid-1800s Masonic leader Albert Pike.[5] Pike merged occult mysticism, the teaching of the German philosopher Hegel and traditional Masonry. Pound, like Pike, was deeply influenced by Hegel's dialectic theory. Hegel said that everything is in a constant state of change. This background undermined any view of God and His absolutes with which Pound might have grown up. Therefore, he was well prepared to accept and then expound and teach the theory that law, like biological species, should and must evolve.

For law to evolve and change required a tremendous departure from the absolutes of the Biblically-based common law and Blackstone-based jurisprudence. Blackstone's Commentaries were the standard of the legal system from the time of the founding until after the Civil War.

Pound's efforts—and their results brought both praise and criticism. One critic summed up Pound's goal this way:

> ...*the jurist should act as an "engineer" to mold society to the ends he thinks proper....constructing legal history (by their decisions) in a way calculated to put their social goals into practice.*[6]

Much of Pound's legal writing, lecturing and teaching was directed to that end. His significant books included *The Spirit of the Common Law, Law and Morals, Social Control Through Law,* and *Law and Liberty*.

As a proponent of *sociological jurisprudence* Pound opposed what he called "Mechanical Jurisprudence." Pound regarded mechanical jurisprudence as applying the law or the Constitution as it was written. For this reason, a disdain for Blackstone and traditional common law teachings runs through Pound's books. In *The Spirit of the Common Law* Pound, in 1921, writes Blackstone off with these words:

> *It was only in the present generation that legal education in the majority of our best schools was divorced from Blackstone....[an] obsolete legal science. (SOTCL-pg. 150)*

Support for almost anything can be found in Pound's works if the researcher is not careful about the overall context. For example, the Internet *World of Quotes*, in its "Historic Quotes and Proverbs Archives," features this seemingly contradictory Pound quote from his 1923 book, *Interpretations of Legal History*:

The law must be stable and yet it must not stand still.

In other words, the law as written is important, but it must evolve. Those words characterize Pound.

Pound's views in his book, *Law and Morals*, on the surface also can be confusing. He advocates that law should evolve or change to uphold *morals*. Pound's position was that the common law upheld *justice* at the expense of *morals*. That could be puzzling. Traditional common law justice was based on scripture and natural law which society generally regarded as right, decent, proper and moral. Why then should it need to "evolve" to uphold morals? As Pound's book unfolds, it becomes obvious that he does not believe that upholding the common law results in what is moral, even though the common law was based on divine revelation and natural law. Pound's view of what is moral is that which man and changing society at any time may believe is right, no matter what God has said (or is alleged to have said). That's why Pound wrote that based on justice...

...legal precepts sometimes are, and perhaps sometimes must be, at variance with the requirements of morals. (LAM pg. 41)

To explain, Pound wrote:

Under the influence of Hegel [to whom Pound refers often], law came to be thought of as an unfolding or a realizing of the idea of right. Legal history was a record of how the idea of right had realized itself progressively in human experience of the ad-ministration of justice. (LAM pg. 16-17)

In other words, because for Hegel and Pound what is "right" or "moral" is in a constant state of change, legal precepts "at times must be at variance with morals." For Pound and Hegel there are no absolutes, no unchanging standards. This was a total upending of the basis of the common law and the precepts on which the *Declaration of Independence* and the Constitution were based. Pound basically rejects the idea that God through His Bible has revealed the principles of law and justice to man. He explains that the long held concept that law came ultimately from God was a theory developed when...

> ...*the natural law jurists, in an age of skepticism, were eager to convince all men upon an unimpeachable basis of reason and thus secure a general adherence to the precepts of the legal order. (LAM pg. 9)*

In other words, to get support and acceptance, those who made the law lied when they told society that "God said...." From this viewpoint, those like Blackstone or the writers of the *Declaration of Independence* also based their work on lies. (Such views permeate many of today's textbooks.)

Pound's expressed attitude and a study of Pound's teachings on Masonry shows that he does not accept the God of the Bible. Under the auspices of the Grand Master of the Massachusetts Masonic Temple in Boston, Pound delivered a series of five lectures on the Philosophy of Masonry. They were published in the April 1915 Masonic magazine, *The Builder*.[7] Of Masonry and Pike's teaching of it, Pound wrote:

> *Masonry....teaches us to save ourselves by finding for ourselves the ultimate principle by which we shall come to the real [Pound also calls "the real," the "Absolute"]....the responsibility of reaching the real through them [Masonic teachings] is upon each of us....But what a feast! It is nothing less than the whole history of human search for reality....And through mastery of it, we shall master the universe.*

That was Pound's life work. The theme of Pound's book *Law and Morals* and his advocacy of *sociological jurisprudence* show how the universe is to be mastered. He sees the goal as...

> ...*transferring (law) from individual interests to social interests. Satisfaction of human wants has been the watchword rather than general security. (LAM pg.109)*

In other words, law must be changed from protecting the individual and his property (as the common law did). The change would be made by subordinating the individual and his rights and property to the wants and needs of society. To do this would require turning aside from the absolutes of the common law and also require discarding the Blackstonian concept that law should be interpreted, understood and applied as "it is written." Traditional principles of law had to be turned upside down to achieve the changes Hegel and Pound looked for.

However, as dedicated as he was to change, Pound was no overnight revolutionary. Realizing that moving too fast could provoke reaction and resistance, Pound cautioned...

> *We must ask how far, if we formulate a precept in terms of our moral principle, it may be made effective in action. Even more we must consider how far it is possible to give the moral principle legal recognition and legal and legal efficacy by juridical action of juristic reasoning, on the basis of the received legal materials and with the received legal technique, without impairing the general security by unsettling the legal system as a whole. (LAM pg. 67)*

In practice, that meant taking a small step in the desired direction and then resting and consolidating what had been achieved before moving on. Pound, like England's Fabian Socialists, knew that moving too quickly could stimulate reaction and resistance. Pound's caution often brought him criticism from more radical legal activists.

In his book, *The Spirit of the Common Law*, Pound really shows that he understood and spelled out the basis of the common law tradition on which America grew great. It is a valuable book for that reason. However, the book also shows his disdain for that tradition. For example, he wrote:

> *On the one hand, it [the common law] is characterized by an extreme individualism. A foreign observer has said that its distinguishing marks are "unlimited valuation of individual liberty and respect for individual property." It is concerned not with social righteousness but with individual rights....it is so zealous to secure fair play to the individual that it often secures very little fair play to the public. (SOTCL pg. 13-14)*

Pound, continuing to speak of the common law, adds:

> *It is jealous of all interference with individual freedom of action, physical, mental, or economic. In short, the isolated individual is*

the center of many of its most significant doctrines. (SOTCL pg. 14)

Instead of requiring that "what is written" in law, contracts, agreements, etc. be fulfilled, Pound held that the law should be lenient. He writes:

Individualism is a prime characteristic of the stage of legal development to which I have referred as strict law. For example, the strict law insists upon full and exact performance at all events of a duty undertaken in legal form. It makes no allowance for accident and has no mercy for defaulters. (SOTCL pg. 18)

By the 21st Century, moving away from "strict law" has filled the courts. The courts are jammed with people who make personal decisions or choices, sign business contracts, enter marriage, etc. Then they sue to get their agreements set aside. They often claim that they are "victims" in some way. They demand compensation for their personal failures to make wise choices.

Of course, there are instances where there can be a total unfairness. That was acknowledged and provided for in the Anglo-American common law tradition. There were courts of equity where a plaintiff could go if there was a total unfairness in application of strict law.

By the time of the founders, much that came from the common law was written, and was regarded as *strict law*. Pound saw Puritanism in 16th and 17th Century England as the influence which formed the spirit of the common law tradition. (SOTCL pg. 36)

The existence of God and His right to rule was the basis of what is called Puritanism. Puritanism, like the God of the Bible, also emphasized that individuals were responsible for their own actions. Those are the reasons it is hated and scorned in today's academic circles.

What were the Puritan standards for which Pound expressed such scorn? Pound detailed the Puritan concepts which he wanted to see "evolve" and change:

No authority might rightfully coerce them (individual choices); but every one must assume and abide the consequences of the choice he made. (SOTCL pg. 42)

The whole (society) is to have no right of control over the individual beyond the minimum necessary to keep the peace. Everything else is to be left to the free contract of a free man....fools who make bad bargains should be held to the consequences of their folly. (SOTCL pg. 49, 53)

The Ten Commandments and Scriptures, interpreted by individual Christians, furnished sufficient general principles. For the rest, there was a need only of local laws to which those subject thereto had freely assented. (SOTCL pg. 54)

Pound says, "Happily this idea passed its meridian in our constitutional law at the end of the last century." What did Pound, writing in the early 20th Century see as the solution to the problems of Puritanism? He wrote:

...it is not the fundamental principles of jurisprudence, but traditional principles of Puritanism, operating out of their sphere, with which American legislatures are struggling. We may abate some of our hostility to legislation, and may be willing to allow lawmakers to take into account the demands involved in social life and formulate in laws the needs of crowded urban industrial communities <u>even in derogation of our traditional law.</u> (Emphasis added.) (SOTCL pg. 58)

Legislators, Pound believed, were to be given power to override traditional law (even if based on the Constitution). But Pound's ultimate goal was giving judges the power to make new laws through their decisions. He writes:

...allow the magistrate some power of meeting the exigencies of justice in concrete cases. We may be willing to trust a trial judge to use honestly and impartially the discretion without which trials will always be dilatory, expensive and unsatisfactory. (SOTCL pg. 58)

Such decisions, under the Case Law process, becomes the new basis of law.

Pound's book, *The Spirit of the Common Law*, gives a good overview of the development of law over the centuries. He just disagrees with the premises on which common law, which he terms strict law, was based. Pound was looking to and working toward the evolving of law.

Sir Edward Coke, a 17th Century English jurist, is known as the "Father of the Common Law." Under Coke's principled brilliance came the doctrine that...

> ...it was the function of the common law and of common-law courts to stand between the individual and oppressive action by the state; that the courts were set up and the law existed to guard individual interests against the encroachments of state and society. (SOTCL pg. 74)

Advocates of social jurisprudence believed that protection of society (as envisioned by the social scientists) has to be supreme even at the expense of the individual and his rights. The U.S. Constitution and its Bill of Rights forbid that concept. Words attributed to Patrick Henry said:

> The Constitution is not an instrument through which the government restrains the people, it is an instrument through which the people restrain government.[8]

Pound disagrees, writing...

> ...Suffice it to say here that if, as I shall try to show on another occasion, the classical juristic theory [the common law] as laid down by Coke and developed in the eighteenth century is untenable and must be abandoned by the jurist. (SOTCL pg. 80)

Pound's goal was rule by judges. That would replace the rule of law established by the consent of the governed. His proposal was revolutionary and frightening. He supports his idea of having judges rule with these words:

> Attempts to reduce the judicial office in the United States to the purely mechanical function of applying rules imposed without and of serving as a mouthpiece for the popular will for the moment are not in the line of progress. (SOTCL pg. 84)

In those words, Pound calls for judges who will rule even though the rulings conflict with established law and "the popular will." Pound's proposals have resulted in what is today regarded by many as "Judicial Tyranny." Pound's philosophical compatriots included Supreme Court Justices Oliver Wendell Holmes, Benjamin Cardozo, and Louis Brandeis.

From his Hegelian perspective, Pound saw and believed that change would come from conflict. Pound envisioned that the conflict which would produce change would come from the clash of two desires. The first was the Puritan concept of individual freedom and responsibility. Puritanism support for individual freedom and responsibility strengthened and grew, Pound said, as men moved west as pioneers. Summed up, the Puritan concept said:

> *If man had to be governed, apart from God and individual conscience, it must be by known rules of law....which would tie down the magistrate by leaving as little as possible to his personal judgment and discretion, leaving as much as possible to the initiative of the individual while keeping all governmental and official action to the minimum required for harmonious coexistence of the individual and of the whole of society. (SOTCL pgs. 119-120)*

With insight, Pound saw that the conflict with such traditional "frontier views" of individual freedom and responsibility came with the development of cities and urban life. He wrote:

> *Men are saying today that material welfare is the great end to which all institutions must be directed and by which they must be measured. Men are not asking merely to be allowed to achieve welfare; they are asking to have welfare achieved for them through organized society. (SOTCL pg. 109)*

In other words, as men came to cities they would be willing to trade their personal freedom to have their material wants satisfied.

There were other philosophical conflicts which factored into the changing of law, justice and culture on which Pound commented. One of them had to do with the view of how law developed. The historical view, as Pound explained, could be summarized this way:

> *Traditionally, the Anglo-American common law concept from Sir Edward Coke, Blackstone, etc. was that law was not made, it was to be discovered. Law ultimately came from God through (1) Biblical divine revelation; (2) in pagan and heathen cultures through God's Romans 2:14-15 work in the hearts of heathen, and (3) through the work of man who discovered law through reason, experience and study of the scriptures.*

Pound disagreed with this concept. He disagreed because such a concept left no room for the law to evolve and change. If law comes from God and is discovered, it is not, therefore, subject to the personal whims of judges, nor the demands of a stirred up pressure group. Pound's disagreement was not the view of one legal revolutionary. He headed the nation's most prestigious law school training future attorneys and judges. What Pound did at Harvard, other law schools soon followed.

Pound's influence expanded through his speeches, lectures, and voluminous correspondence with U.S. Presidents, Supreme Court justices, judges, and most of the prominent legal figures from 1910 through the 1950s.

Even with all of that influence, Pound admitted that deceit and guile would be necessary. Deceit and guile were essential if judges were to make the changes in law and the culture, the ultimate goal of Pound and the advocates of sociological jurisprudence. Pound told why deceit and guile would be required when judges came up with new law. He realized that if judges tried to change the law, while men still understood the traditional views of law, people would...

> *...insist upon knowing where the pre-existing rule was to be found before judges discovered and applied it, in what form it existed, and how and whence it derived its form and obtained it authority. And when as a result of such inquiries, the rule seems to have sprung full fledged from the judicial head, the assumption that the judicial function is one of interpretation and application only leads to the conclusion that the courts are exercising a usurped authority. (SOTCL pg. 171)*

What was Pound's answer? How are the absolutes of the law to be overturned? He wrote:

> *If all legal rules are contained in immutable form in holy writ or in twelve tables or in a code or in received corpus juris or in the custom of the realm [laws of nature] whose principles are authoritatively evidenced, not only must new situations be met by deduction and analogical extension under the guise of interpretation but the inevitable changes to which all law is subject must be hidden under the same guise. (SOTCL pg. 171)*

Pound was maintaining that while laws or the interpretation of them may be changed, the form must be kept the same. He says:

> In each case the result was infusion of morals [by his definition that's what people or someone wants] into law and a making over of the law, <u>although in theory the old rules stood unaltered.</u> (Emphasis added.) (SOTCL pg. 172)

Pound tells how it could be done. He wrote:

> Law grows more or less...surreptitiously under the cloak of fictions [lies?]. Next it grows consciously but shamefacedly through general fictions [made up reasons]. Finally, it may grow consciously, deliberately and avowed through juristic science and legislation tested by judicial empiricism. (SOTCL pg. 173)

As the law "grew," Pound spelled out the result of the change. On page 13 of his book, *Law and Morals*, he wrote:

> ...the state is the unchallengeable authority behind legal precepts. The state takes the place of Jehovah handing down the tables of the law to Moses.

This is exactly what has happened to the Constitution of the United States under the pressures of sociological jurisprudence.

Pound wrote his words over 80 years ago. Today, so few Americans have any understanding of our true legal traditions and constitutional history that few men...

> ...insist upon knowing where the pre-existing rule was to be found before judges discovered and applied it, in what form it existed, and how and where it derived its form and obtained its authority.

Eighty years have passed since Pound acknowledged that the American people's knowledge of law and tradition was an obstacle to judges making new law. American schools, under the influence of Pound's contemporary John Dewey, have dumbed down successive generations of Americans. Most no longer recognize the difference between what had been written and established and what judges say is law.

What has resulted? In the next to last chapter of his book, *The Spirit of the Common Law*, Pound said:

> Eight noteworthy changes in the law in the present generation....have been taking place almost unnoticed, and a shifting

was in progress in our case law from the individualist justice of the nineteenth century, which has passed so significantly by the name of legal justice, to the social justice of today <u>even before the change in our legislative policy became so marked</u>. (Emphasis added) (SOTCL pg. 185)

The eight changes Pound saw developing have produced drastic changes in American culture, families and way of life. Pound's changes included:

1. ...limitations on the use of property to prevent anti-social exercise of ownership and accomplish "the interests of society." (SOTCL pg. 185)

A blatant limitation on private property rights came as the Supreme Court ended its 2004-2005 session. The decision in *Kelo v. City of New London* ruled that cities can use the power of eminent domain to seize private property (people's homes, small businesses, etc.) Private developments which would produce more tax revenue can then be given the use of the property. This is a full blown sociological jurisprudence decision. Private property rights which were upheld by the common law and the Constitution have been abolished "for the good of society." The Supreme Court's decision basically eliminates the clear property rights provision of the 5th Amendment. That provision allows taking of private property (with compensation) when it is needed for "public use"—building a road, utility lines, etc.—but not for other private owners to use. For many "eminent domain" is an abstract concept *until* a developer and a city government combine to take the homes and small businesses of dozens or hundreds of people. Those who have lived in their homes for much of their lives are uprooted "for the good of society."

2. Limitations upon the freedom of contract have been designed by the courts and legislatures to protect those who are subjected to economic pressure and unfair advantage on the part of those who have greater economic power. (SOTCL pgs. 186-187)

Rights to freely *contract* (make agreements) have been limited by wage and hour laws, compulsory unionism, etc.

3. Pound saw courts putting limitations on the power of a creditor or injured party to secure what is due them if it places hardships on the "victims." (SOTCL pgs. 187-188)

Today, limitations are imposed by law on efforts to collect bad debts and require individuals to face responsibilities.

4. Pound advocated that where there is no blame on either side, social justice will ask, "Who can best bear the loss?" (SOTCL pgs.188-189)

Today, there is "no fault insurance" and "no fault divorce." No fault divorces have multiplied single family households.

5. Pound said that natural resources such as running water and wild game are assets of society which are not capable of private appropriation or ownership except under regulations that protect the social interest. (SOTCL pg. 189)

Court oversight of environmental rules is an example.

6. Pound foresaw the day when Courts should no longer make the natural rights of the parents the chief basis of court decisions with respect to children and their rearing, their education, etc. (SOTCL pg. 189)

Today, the "law" and the views of social scientists have replaced many Bible guidelines for the rearing, training and disciplining of children. Parents can't keep their minor children from getting abortions. One court granted a teenager's request to "divorce" his parents. The boy didn't like the religious training his parents were giving him. States have usurped parental rights in a myriad of ways.

To achieve these goals Pound said a body of law must be developed by judges...

...which will satisfy the demands of society today...apart from the ultra-individualist materials of eighteenth century jurisprudence and nineteenth century common law... (SOTCL pg.190)

Some changes can be beneficial and may help society and individuals. However, such changes should be made legislatively rather than through judge-made law.

Ideas have consequences. Bad ideas, when accepted or even tolerated, can have tragic results. Broken homes, multitudes of babies born out of wedlock, school districts where half of the children come from broken homes are a few of the tragic results of widespread acceptance of Pound's sociological jurisprudence. AIDs and rampant growth of other sexually-transmitted diseases are another.

SEX RESEARCHER KINSEY'S FINDINGS SPURRED MOVE TO REPLACE COMMON LAW WITH CODE LAW

Alfred Kinsey's research was contrived, ideologically driven and misleading. Any judge, legislator or other public official who gives credence to that research is guilty of malpractice and dereliction of duty.

Charles E. Rice
Professor of Law, Notre Dame

TO ACHIEVE SOCIOLOGICAL JURISPRUDENCE the common law had to be replaced with *code law*. The agency by which it was accomplished were the "findings" of sex researcher Alfred Kinsey in the 1940s and 1950s which "proved" that law must be changed. To understand the real reason for the change it is necessary to know the difference between the common law and code law.

Traditional common law and code law differ in that the two types of "law" get their authority from different sources. Understanding the difference is important. The two types are:

The common law, as spelled out by Blackstone in his Commentaries, was based on Judaic-Christian principles. It looked to God as the ultimate authority. It was stable—it could not evolve. Any "law" which violated God's revealed law was invalid. (America law and justice from the beginning were common law based.)

The authority for Code law came, not from God, but from statutes enacted by legislatures. Increasingly code law has also developed from bureaucratic regulations authorized by legislatures. Codes can change anytime the legislature or the bureaucrats want to make a change.

Replacing the common law with codes was the result of what Roscoe Pound was seeing in 1924 when he wrote:

...the state is the unchallengeable authority behind legal precepts. The state takes the place of Jehovah handing down the tables of the law to Moses.

On that basis, code law can change anytime the state wants the law to change. Therefore, code law has no stability, creating unrest in society.

Using the theories of "social scientists," the American Law Institute (ALI) pushed legislatures to replace the common law with "code" law. Established in 1923 with Rockefeller Foundation financing, the ALI's stated purpose was to...

...to promote the clarification and simplification of the law and its better adaptation to social needs....The Institute drafts and publishes various Restatements of the Law, Model Codes and other proposals for law reform.[1]

Since the 1950s, major efforts have resulted in developing the ALI's Model Penal Code (MPC), the Uniform Commercial Code, the Principles of the Law of Family Dissolution, and a myriad of other legal "reforms." The effort goes on.

The American Legislative Exchange Council (ALEC) is a 2,400-member organization of state legislators. ALEC did a four-year study on the impact of ALI Model Penal Code on America's justice system, laws and culture. The 120-page report was completed in 2004. A comprehensive 16-page summary is titled *Restoring Legal Protections for Women and Children: A Historical Analysis of the States' Criminal Codes.[2]* ALEC said ALEC commissioned the study...

...because of the widespread use of "junk science" misdirecting legislatures, courts and education.[3] The "junk science" adopted by most state legislatures was based on Indiana University's Kinsey Reports (1948, 1953).

The ALEC study showed that the American Law Institute's Model Penal Code was "sold" to judges, attorneys and state legislators using the "research" of Alfred Kinsey, a "sex researcher" at the University of Indiana. Kinsey's work more than that of any other "social scientist" of the 20th Century undermined laws supporting traditional morality, marriage and children. The ALEC report charged that...

...specific protections were lost [from the law] for American women and children based on widespread legislative and judicial reliance upon the Kinsey Reports and the American Law Institute's Model Penal Code [MPC].

Kinsey was trained as a zoologist but in 1942 he became head of the Institute for Research in Sex, Gender and Reproduction at the University of Indiana. The Kinsey Institute was jointly sponsored and financed by the Rockefeller Foundation and the National Research Council.

Kinsey's 1948 book, *Sexual Behavior of the Human Male,* produced by the Institute rocked the nation. The book got rave reviews in *Time, Newsweek,* and the leading newspapers of the day. Over 500,000 copies were sold, 200,000 of them in two months. Overnight, Kinsey became a national hero and was featured on the cover of *TIME* magazine. In 1953, he published a follow up, *Sexual Behavior of the Human Female.* [4]

The *Kinsey Reports* and the books he based on them reported that...

...95% of all men and almost half of all women have premarital sex....50% of men and 40% of women are unfaithful in marriage....71% of the women claimed that their infidelity had not harmed their marriages and some even said it had helped.

The "statistics" Kinsey developed in his research and cited in his books went on and on. For example, Kinsey reported that...

...40% of all men have had some homosexual experiences and at least 10% of men have been homosexuals over a period of at least three years. [5]

Kinsey's "statistics" on widespread homosexuality in America are used today by the homosexual community in an attempt to gain acceptance. In the area of perversion, Kinsey also claimed that his research showed that...

..17% of all boys who grew up on farms had experienced sex with animals. [6]

America's trusted public institutions and professions adopted the Kinsey Report's radical findings. Kinsey said that under the 1948 common law state criminal codes 95% of "normal" American men would be classified as sex offenders. These Kinsey "sex offenders" were the World War II veterans of "the greatest generation." Based on his statistics, Kinsey campaigned for "science-based legal reform" to keep up with man's "evolution."[7]

CRISIS magazine's May 2004 article said that at a 1955 conference sponsored by Planned Parenthood, Kinsey pulled a "statistical bombshell out of his hat." Kinsey said that his research showed in the 1940s and 1950s that...

...of all pregnant women, roughly 50% of singles and 25% of those who were married aborted their babies. A whopping 87% of those abortions were performed by bona fide doctors.[8]

With these "facts," Kinsey gave scientific authority to the notion that abortion was already a common procedure and should be legalized. The Supreme Court did the same less than twenty years later in the *Roe v. Wade* decision.

Was Kinsey's research valid? Some prominent critics warned that it was flawed. Critics included noted anthropologist Margaret Mead (not known as a conservative or moralist), Karl Menninger, M.D. of the famed Menninger Institute, and noted Stanford Psychiatrist Lewis Terman.[9] There were enough concerns that the Rockefeller Foundation quietly withdrew its $100,000 annual support for Kinsey's Institute.[10] But the damage was already done.

Kinsey's "research" and his books have had a continuing impact on both the culture and the law. The support the Kinsey studies gave to the idea that "everyone is doing it," helped produce the 1960s sexual revolution. Even Playboy Magazine's founder, Hugh Hefner, gave Kinsey the "credit" for fostering the sexual revolution. Kinsey's claimed that 10% of the male population was either actively homosexual or latently homosexual. That claim became the basis for the homosexual revolution as well. Society is still suffering. The attitude that "if everyone is doing it, it must be OK" violates the Biblical admonition in Exodus 23:2 which says:

Thou shalt not follow a multitude to do evil.

Kinsey's "research" was used to "sell" the American Law Institutes Model Penal Code to State legislators between 1960 and 1980. Dr. Linda Jeffrey, director of the ALEC study, and Eunice Ray of RSVP America concluded that the ALI Model Penal Code was deceptively introduced to bar associations, law schools, attorneys and judges as merely...

> ...a codification of our common law with a few changes reflecting up-to-date developments in law, based upon the "social science experts" whose role in law was beginning to challenge and replace that of judge and jury.[11]

The actual result was not just codifying the common law. *The common law was actually replaced and common law crimes were abolished.* That claim was spelled out and acknowledged in the 1962 draft of the American Law Institute's Model Penal Code.[12]

Replacing the Biblically-based common law was Kinsey's goal. Kinsey's 1997 sympathetic biographer James Jones revealed that Kinsey's vision was...

> ...to end the sexual repression of our English-American common law traditions.[13]

That charge had support even from President Bill Clinton's Georgetown University mentor, Dr. Carroll Quigley. In his classic book, *Tragedy and Hope—A History of The World in Our Time,* Quigley said that...

> ...the Rockefeller Foundation-sponsored Kinsey Report was deliberately designed as an attack on Judaic-Christian morality.[14]

Acceptance and use of Kinsey's "work" was the ultimate triumph of the proposals of Roscoe Pound and his sociological jurisprudence advocates. They transformed America's legal system. Between 1960 and 1980, the legislatures of over thirty states adopted the ALI *Model Penal Code* in various forms. A study done by *RSVP America* showed that common law protections for marriage, women and children were abolished or trivialized. They included:

> *Fornication, adultery and cohabitation were decriminalized....divorce has been made easy and thereby frequent....parental responsibility and support have been replaced with welfare programs which make the taxpayers "daddy" to multitudes of children born out of wedlock....government sponsored contraception and abortion programs are provided to teenagers without parental knowledge or approval....rape has been redefined to*

include a range of crimes which can be plea bargained down to misdemeanors such as "sexual misconduct."....sodomy which was a criminal act in every state in 1961 is now legal and constitutional in all States with sodomites having access to classrooms and the White House. [15]

Was Kinsey's research, on which the transformation of America's criminal law system was based, valid? It took years before someone was dedicated enough to really dig into Kinsey's research methods and personal morals.

Dr. Judith Reisman, a Ph.D. and psychologist, spent years researching Kinsey's methods and life. She produced a series of books. [16] Reisman's book, *Kinsey: Crimes & Consequences*, a bestseller, is currently available. Her first book, *Kinsey, Sex and Fraud* was published in 1990. It was reviewed by the internationally respected British Medical Journal, *The Lancet*. The review said her book shows that Kinsey...

...has left his former co-workers some explaining to do. [17]

Facts were uncovered which showed Kinsey was both a pervert and a total fraud as a researcher. His sympathetic biographer James H. Jones revealed that Kinsey was a sado-masochistic homosexual on a perverted mission. In their books, Jones and other former associates detailed Kinsey's homosexual encounters. He encouraged wife swapping sessions among key staff members. [18]

Reisman charged that an overwhelming percentage of the people Kinsey and his associates interviewed were prison inmates, sex offenders, prostitutes and other dysfunctional people. Kinsey's research also involved illegal sexual experimentation by nine pedophiles on several hundred children, some as young as two months. Based on their "experiments," Kinsey proclaimed that children were sexual from birth. Several Kinsey research associates were interviewed in a 1998 British television documentary. They confirmed Kinsey's use of pedophiles. Shown by the BBC, the shocking program, titled, *Secret Histories: Kinsey's Paedophiles,* has never been aired on network TV in America. [19]

Most such charges had already been revealed in 1979 by Kinsey's co-author, Paul Gebhard. Kinsey claimed that his book, *Sexual Behavior of the Human Male*, was based on 18,000 interviews. After

Kinsey's death, co-author Paul Gebhard became the Kinsey Institute Director. Gebhard undertook to "update" the figures in 1979. He reported that instead of the claimed 18,000 interviews of "average American males," Kinsey's research really was based on only...

> ...5,300 white males. Of the 5,300, 2,446 were convicts, 1,003 were homosexuals, 50 were transvestites, 117 were mentally ill, 342 were classified "Other," and 650 had been sexually abused as boys. Only 873 actual "normal" male subjects were among those who were interviewed.[20]

Kinsey's "scientific research" based on those figures largely shaped Western Society's beliefs and understanding of the nature of human sexuality for the last half century. *CRISIS* magazine said...

> In short, Kinsey's team researched the most exotic sexual behavior in America—taking hundreds if not thousands of case histories from sexual deviants—and then passed the behavior off as sexually "normal," "natural," and "average" (and hence socially and morally acceptable.[21]

In 1954, a special committee of Congress headed by Tennessee Congressman Carroll Reece of Tennessee examined the influence of tax-exempt foundations in transforming American culture. The study focussed particular attention on how foundation grants supported the work of radical revolutionaries in the social sciences. The committee report found that among the social scientists...

> ...there are no absolutes, that everything is indeterminate, that no standards of conduct, morals, ethics, and government are deemed to be inviolate, that everything, including basic moral law, is subject to change, and that it is the part of the social scientists to take no principle for granted as a premise in social or judicial reasoning, however fundamental it may hereto have been deemed to be under our Judaic-Christian moral system.[22]

That statement characterized the teachings of the "social scientists." On such work, Roscoe Pound advocated building the new system of Sociological Jurisprudence. Kinsey's "research" was the "social science" used in transforming laws which once had supported traditional morality.

Once Kinsey's books skyrocketed to fame, the American Law Institute efforts to move America's justice system away from its common law base were moved to the front burner.

The ALI Model Penal Code was "sold" to legislators in over thirty states through State Law Journals. During the 1950 to 1980 period, law journals cited the Kinsey Report data to...

> ...advocate legalizing prostitution (Maine, 1976); harmlessness of boy prostitution (Duke University, 1960); lightening sex crime penalties (Ohio, 1959); legalizing homosexuality (South Dakota, 1968); the need for "beneficent concerns for pedophiles" (Georgia, 1969); and for general sex law revisions (Oklahoma, 1970). Law journals commonly cited the Kinsey "facts" that 95% of males are sex offenders (Oregon 1972); that young children are seducers (Missouri, 1973) and that juridical bias is the cause of "severe condemnation of sex offenders" (Pennsylvania, 1952).[23]

Dr. Linda Jeffrey was the Chief Author of the ALEC Report. Dr. Judith Reisman was the Scientific Advisor to the Subcommittee on Junk Science. The authors use the actual words of the ALI *Model Penal Code* authors to expose their philosophy, goals and aims. That makes the ALEC Report an invaluable resource. For example, Louis B. Schwartz, author of the "Sex Offense" section of the Model Penal Code denied that sexual perversion was an evil. His rambling words in the *University of Pennsylvania Law Review* in 1948 said:

> To reveal that certain behavior patterns are widespread, that they are a product of environment, opportunity, age and other factors over which the individual has little control, that they are not objectively harmful except as a result of society's efforts at repression, to suggest that the law ought not to punish and the psychiatrists might better devote themselves to reassuring the sexual deviate rather than giving attention to "redirect behavior"—all these add up to a denial that sexual "perversion" is an evil.[24]

Schwartz then pictured "the distant day when Americans cease to regard minority morals as a legitimate object of social coercion." He suggested this covert method for changing state criminal codes:

> Eventually, such distinctions ease themselves into the written law, especially if it can be done in the course of a general revision

*of the penal code. This avoids the appearance of outright repudia-
tion of Conservative moral standards [and the common law], by
presenting the changes in a context of merely technical improve-
ments.*[25]

Schwartz proposes deceit and guile, as Roscoe Pound, explained
in Chapter VI, said would be necessary to get sociological
jurisprudence into the law. Schwartz said dramatic changes in laws
based on morals should be presented as merely technical changes
in the law.

The ALEC report said this created a crisis in American law...

*...because modern evolving law, supposedly based on science,
conflicted with America's long settled (and protective) common
law which "experts" portrayed as inconsistent, ambiguous, outmoded and redundant.*[26]

By definition, law, to be "law," must be fixed. However, state
commissions revised state penal *codes* according to the new ALI
MPC's understanding that law constantly evolves and requires
constant change. The ALEC Report quoted an evaluation of the
Kinsey Reports impact on American law by the acting Dean of
Indiana University Frank Horack, Jr. Horack said:

*The principal impact of the Kinsey Report will be at the level of
the administration of the law. It will provide the statistical
support which police officers, prosecutors, judges, probation officers and superintendents of penal institutions need for judging
individual cases...Officers will read it. Defense counsel will cite
it. Even when not entered into evidence, it will condition official
action. Psychiatrists, psychologists, penologists, juvenile and
probation officers all participate in modern penal procedures—
they will use the data and their professional advice will be heeded
by the judge.*[27]

Kinsey personally worked on "the revision of sex laws," with
commissions in Illinois, New Jersey, New York, Delaware, Wyoming
and Oregon.[28] In December 1949, Kinsey testified for an entire day
before the "California Subcommittee on Sex Crimes." Kinsey
reviewed his work and told the committee:

*...we find that 95 per cent of the [male] population has in actuality
engaged in sexual activities, which are contrary to the law.*[29]

As a solution, Kinsey advocated weakening or replacing laws which protected traditional morality, marriage and children—replacing the common law with code law.

The Model Penal Code revised the definition of criminal responsibility, using the guidance of three psychiatrists. Traditionally, the M'Naughten Rule dating back to 1843 required that an offender know right and wrong in order to be guilty of crime. The drafters of the Model Penal Code thought that in addition to knowledge of right and wrong, the offender's capacity for self-control must be determined. Did the offender have the ability to conform to the law.[30] Such revolutionary changes have effected attitudes about a criminal's responsibility and punishment for the criminal act. The *St. Louis Post-Dispatch* February 1, 2005 reported:

> *A federal judge took mercy Monday on a 36 year old woman who embezzled more that $350,000, shaving months off the required prison term because she had suffered sexual abuse as a child. Her defense attorney said she deserved a break because she had endured abuse as a child, starting at age 8 and had tried to compensate for low self esteem by buying more things than she could afford.*[31]

The federal judge who reduced her sentence apparently agreed. Benjamin Karpman perhaps told why. Karpman is quoted as the primary psychiatric authority in the Model Penal Code. He claimed that criminal behavior could be compared to tonsillitis, saying:

> *Criminal behavior is an unconsciously conditional psychic reaction over which [the criminals] have no conscious control. We have to treat them as psychically sick people, which in every respect they are. It is no more reasonable to punish these individuals...than it is to punish an individual for breathing through his mouth because of enlarged adenoids, when a simple operation will do the trick.*[32]

The chief author of the ALI Model Penal Code was Columbia University Law Professor Herbert Wechsler. In a *Harvard Law Review* article Wechsler called for revision of common law-based criminal laws of the States. He called common law-based criminal laws "ineffective, inhumane and thoroughly unscientific." He added that...

...the common law "employs unsound psychological premises such as freedom of will or belief that punishment deters."[33]

California Senator Ray Haynes' introduction to the ALEC report pointed to another tragic result of the Kinsey-influenced work of the American Law Institute. He wrote:

> *The ALI penal law reforms recommended to legislators... permitted Kinsey's abnormal sexual conduct to be taught to American children via sex education. Since then public health costs from sexual disease and dysfunction have skyrocketed—indeed all measures of socio-sexual disorder have soared from the 1960s [when sex education was widely adopted in America's schools] and when protective laws began to be weakened and/or eliminated.*[34]

Judith Reisman's book points out that Kinsey's conclusions have become the basis for school sex education programs. They are taught at every level of education from elementary school to college. Kinsey's claims, Reisman says, are presented in textbooks as undisputed truth.

The sexual revolution has produced tragic results. Several generations of homes, marriages and children have suffered. Some aspects of the sufferings were documented in the 2002 book, *Epidemic: How Teen Sex Is Killing Our Kids,*[35] written by teen pediatric specialist, Dr. Meg Meeker. Her book says that:

> *Nearly 1 in 5 adolescents is living with a sexually transmitted disease....In the 1960s, a shot of penicillin could cure the two known STD's, syphilis and gonorrhea. Today, there are at least 25 STD's without simple cures and in most cases there are no cures at all....Over 80% of STD-infected teens are unaware they have an STD; therefore they don't get medical attention and may continue to infect others....False claims are made in sex education materials which under inform or mislead kids about STD's and condoms which offer little or no protection from disease....Pharmaceutical companies promote drugs that control STD symptoms, encouraging kids in the delusion that they can be promiscuous without any associated problems....Anatomic and immunological differences make the adolescent body—particularly the females'—more susceptible to STD's than the adult body....*[36]

The report of the 2,400-member American Legislative Exchange Council in conclusion asks: *How Should Legislators Respond?* The report recommended five actions legislators should consider.[37] They include:

1. Legislators should develop and make presentations to inform those in leadership of the history and scope of Kinsey's fraudulent "science-based reforms."

2. The legal reforms that have been enacted since 1960 must be examined. Legislators should determine what benefit or detriment these sex law changes have brought to America's law abiding citizens, especially our vulnerable children. Finally, legislators must develop a working system to better protect women and children. The current system is moving society in the wrong direction.

3. Laws must be refocused on illegal acts and their consequences. Criminal behavior must once again be met with criminal sanctions that depend on the act of the aggressor—not the age of the victim or the personality of the offender.

4. State legislatures must require accountability for programs involving rehabilitation. Programs must reduce recidivism or meet other measurable criteria established by the legislature to continue receiving taxpayer support.

5. Undoing harmful changes in sex education curricula is essential. State legislators should continue to call for and work toward accurate science in children's education. A review board should monitor textbooks purchased in all school districts. Concerns of parents should be taken seriously and investigated. Political ideologies should never be represented as science to vulnerable school children.

Advocates of sociological jurisprudence have replaced traditional, Bible-based common law with *code law* based on the teachings of social scientists. The legal system and the culture have been transformed. Tragedies have resulted.

COURTS USE 14TH AMENDMENT TO DESTROY STATE SOVEREIGNTY, NEGATING 9TH & 10TH AMENDMENTS

*All persons born or naturalized in the United States and subject to the juris-
diction thereof, are citizens of the United States and of the State wherein
they reside. No State shall make or enforce any law which shall abridge
the privileges or immunities of citizens of the United States; nor shall any
State deprive any person of life, liberty or property, without due process of
law; nor deny to any person within its jurisdiction the equal protection of
laws.*

*The Congress shall have power to enforce this article by appropriate legis-
lation.*

—Amendment 14: Sections One and Five

FEW AMERICANS TODAY REALIZE that when the Bill of
Rights were added to the Constitution in 1791 they did not apply to
the States. The Bill of Rights were added to the Constitution to
protect the people and the States from the federal government. Most
States already had protections for their citizens in their own constitutions.

That the Bill of Rights had no application in the States and to
State laws and actions was affirmed by the Supreme Court itself in
1833. In *Barron v. Baltimore,* the justices ruled that the Bill of
Rights is...

...not applicable to and do[es] not bind the States.[3]

That was the law for 150 years. Then the U.S. Supreme Court
reversed that decision and "decided" that the Bill of Rights should
apply to the States. Since 1950, the Court has used that interpretation of the 14th Amendment to give Washington control over much
of America. Control of schools, elections, the criminal justice systems, abortion, school prayer, and public acknowledgment of God,
have moved from the States to Washington and its courts.

Elbridge Gerry, a signer of the Declaration and a member of the first Congress explained why the Bill of Rights was not meant to apply to the States. He told Congress:

> *This declaration of rights, I take it, is designed to secure the people against the maladministration of the federal Government.*[1]

In presenting the Bill of Rights for adoption by Congress James Madison said that because State Constitutions already restrained States from interfering with the rights of their citizens...

> *...there is like reason for restraining the Federal Government.*[2]

That the Bill of Rights only applied to the federal government should be obvious from history. A number of the States which adopted those first ten amendments themselves had, at the time, state-supported and state-approved churches. The First Amendment only said that *Congress* could make no law establishing a religion or restricting its free exercise. That applied only to the federal government.

Liberals generally liked the changes which resulted when the Supreme Court through its interpretation of the 14th Amendment imposed federal control on the States and their citizens. Those who didn't included many in the legal profession. They, however, surrendered. They wrongly took the attitude that once the Supreme Court had spoken, the Court's decisions became "the supreme law of the land." The attitude that decisions of the Supreme Court become the "Supreme law of the land" is widely accepted but has no support in the U.S. Constitution. Article VI specifies that only the Constitution itself, the laws of the United States made in conformity to the Constitution and treaties made under the authority of the United States are the Supreme Law of the land.

Younger "scholars" who had grown up in the "living constitution" culture applauded what the Court was doing. Typical was Akhil R. Amar, a prominent law professor at Yale University. In a voluminous essay published in the *Yale Law Journal* in 1992, Amar said:

> *...both the text of Section One [of the Fourteenth Amendment] and the public gloss Congress placed upon the text [when it was*

*passed] made clear that what Congress was proposing was noth-
ing less than a transformation of the original Bill of Rights.*[4]

One scholar did not fall in line so quickly. Raoul Berger, a veteran
law professor at Harvard and the University of California at
Berkeley, called Amar's view "a truly wild flight of fancy." Berger
was a fascinating individual whose love and respect for the Constitution overrode his personal politics. He described his personal
convictions and beliefs as "the standard political principles of the
moderate left of the Democratic Party." His early books on...

*...executive privilege, the death penalty and impeachment made
him an icon in liberal circles. That all changed. Berger became a
hero to constitutional conservatives after he wrote Government By
Judiciary. It was issued in 1977 and quickly produced an on-
going storm of criticism.*[5]

Berger's 555-page book, *Government By Judiciary* is a comprehensive analysis of the transformation of America's governmental structure and society. The transformation resulted from the
Supreme Court's warped interpretation of the Fourteenth Amendment. Berger's detailed notes and references often cover half pages
in the book. They are themselves a historical treasure. In a sup-
plementary introduction to the reissue of the book just before his
95th birthday, Berger wrote:

*It is the thesis of this book that the Supreme Court is not em-
powered to rewrite the Constitution, that in its transformation of
the Fourteenth Amendment it has demonstrably done so. Thereby
the Justices, who are virtually unaccountable, irremovable, and
irreversible, have taken over from the people the control of their
own destiny, an awesome exercise of power.*[6]

How did such a judicial seizure of control come about? As a part
of the Reconstruction efforts following the Civil War, the 13th, 14th
and 15th Amendments were added to the Constitution. They were
adopted to insure that States could not deny former slaves certain
basic rights as citizens. The pertinent sections of the three amendments banned slavery, defined citizenship, and prohibited states
from interfering with the rights of their new citizens who were
primarily the former slaves. The amendments protected the former
slaves right to due process, life, liberty and property, equal protec-

tion of the laws and voting. Other citizens already had these protections as they were understood and enforced at the time.

Starting in about 1950, the Supreme Court in a series of decisions, selectively and progressively, ruled that the "due process" language of the Fourteenth Amendment imposed the First Amendment and other parts of the Bill of Rights on the States. The Supreme Court action is called *incorporation*.[4] The process of *incorporation* puts the Bill of Rights into the "privileges, immunities, due process, and equal protection of the law" which the Fourteenth Amendment forbids States to deny or abridge.

For many years after the Fourteenth Amendment was adopted that wasn't so. The Supreme Court in the famous *Slaughter-House Cases* (1872) resisted efforts to use the Fourteenth Amendment and Fifteenth Amendments to restrict the rights of States to manage their own affairs. In that case, Justice Fields reaffirmed Jefferson's view of the "wall of separation" between the states and the federal government. He wrote...

> ...we do not see in those amendments any purpose to destroy the main features of the general [federal / state] system. Under the pressure of all the excited feeling growing out of the war, our statesmen have still believed that the existence of the states with power for domestic and local government...was essential to the working of our complex form of government.[7]

The Supreme Court held to that position for over 50 years. The first such ruling which overturned that precedent came with the 1925 decision in *Gitlow v. New York*. Benjamin Gitlow had been convicted under New York state law of the crime of criminal anarchy. As a member of the Communist Workers Party Gitlow...

> ...had been responsible for distributing 16,000 copies of Manifesto which advocated "in plain and unequivocal language" the necessity of accomplishing the "Communist Revolution" by a..."revolutionary mass action for the purpose of conquering and destroying the parliamentary state and establishing in its place, through a 'revolutionary dictatorship of the proletariat' the system of Communist Socialism."[8]

The Supreme Court overruled the New York state court criminal anarchy convictions and set Gitlow free. The decision said that the New York state statute...

> ...*deprived the defendant of his liberty of expression <u>in violation of the due process clause of the Fourteenth Amendment</u>....*[9]

The Gitlow decision, in effect, applied the First Amendment's freedom of speech provision and the Supreme Court interpretation of it to the States. It also broadened the definition of speech. Since then federal courts have overturned state convictions of those who have burned the U.S. flag, defecated on historic monuments, created "art" by immersing the crucifix in a jar of urine, etc. Those who did such acts, the courts have said, were "exercising their freedom of speech."

However, with that one decision in 1925 followed by a flood of others since 1950, the Supreme Court has torn down the *wall of separation*. It was the wall the founders designed to protect the States from federal domination. A series of on-going 14th Amendment decisions transferred control over schools, elections, voting, the makeup of state legislatures, administration of criminal justice procedures, the death penalty, and more from the States and people to Washington. State laws which allowed school prayer and Bible reading and those which banned abortion and the practice of sodomy were declared unconstitutional. Those transfers of power to Washington ignored the foundational truth that the federal government was created by the states. Washington was to have no power or authority except the very limited powers given to it by the States.

Thomas Jefferson, foresaw the dangers of a runaway federal court system. In an 1821 letter to Charles Hammond he wrote:

> *...the germ of dissolution of our Federal Government is in the constitution of the Federal judiciary—an irresponsible body...advancing its noiseless step like a thief over the field of jurisdiction until all shall be usurped from the States and the government be consolidated into one. To this I am opposed.*[10]

In another 1823 letter Jefferson was warning:

> *There is no danger I apprehend so much as the consolidation of our government by the noiseless and therefore unalarming instrumentality of the Supreme Court.*[11]

What Jefferson feared has all resulted from the Supreme Court's misinterpretation or misapplication of the 14th Amendment. The Supreme Court has totally ignored the specific words and original intent of those who wrote, debated, passed and adopted the 14th Amendment. Those in the 39th Congress who passed the 14th Amendment specifically promised that the Amendment had nothing to do with control of schools, voting and elections. But their original intent was ignored by the Supreme Court in the 1950s and 1960s.

The change went into high gear after California's Earl Warren was appointed Chief Justice of the U.S. Supreme Court.

LIMITING THE FREE EXERCISE OF RELIGION

The traditional "wall of separation" between the States and the federal government fell when the Supreme Court "incorporated" the Bill of Rights into the 14th Amendment. That opened the door for federal courts to overrule long standing state laws which permitted prayer and Bible reading in the schools. For example, in *Engel v. Vitale (1962)* the Supreme Court decision banning prayer in New York state schools was justified with these words:

> ...*the prohibition of the First Amendment against the enactment of any law "respecting an establishment of religion," <u>...was made applicable to the States by the Fourteenth Amendment...</u>* [12] *(Emphasis added)*

A year later the Supreme Court in *Abington v. Schempp (1963)* struck down a Pennsylvania law under which each school day started with Bible reading and prayer. The decision used the 14th Amendment in the same way. The decision said:

> *Because of the prohibition of the First Amendment against the enactment by Congress of any law "respecting an establishment of religion," <u>which is made applicable to the States by the Fourteenth Amendment,</u> no state law or school board may require that passages from the Bible be read or that the Lord's Prayer be recited in the public schools of a State...* [13] *(Emphasis added)*

In both decisions the Supreme Court recognized that the Bill of Rights did not originally apply to the States. They were only made applicable by the Court's interpretation of the 14th Amendment. Supreme Court Justice Antonin Scalia spoke at Concordia Seminary in St. Louis. Asked whether the *incorporation* doctrine required applying the First Amendment to the States. Scalia replied:

> *That's what the Court said....The Court has interpreted that as essentially applying the Bill of Rights against the States. And not the whole Bill of Rights, just some of the Bill of Rights, essentially those provisions we like.*[14]

The seriousness and impact of the Supreme Court's incorporation doctrine was shown by Wake Forest University Law School professor Michael Curtis. In an essay he said:

> *Without the incorporation doctrine...most of the Supreme Court's First Amendment jurisprudence would not exist.*[15]

Jefferson and the founding fathers, including those who adopted the First Amendment to the Constitution, foresaw the danger of runaway courts. The founders gave the federal government no power over religion. In 1808 Jefferson wrote:

> *Certainly, <u>no power to prescribe any religious exercise or to assume authority in religious discipline has been delegated to the General Government.</u> It must rest with the States, as far as it can be in any human authority.*[16] *(Emphasis added)*

That was Jefferson's understanding of the phrase "separation of church and state" the term he used in the widely misquoted letter. President Jefferson foresaw the danger exactly, mentioning religion earlier in an 1801 letter to the Rhode Island legislature. Jefferson explained the "wall of separation" between the federal and state governments this way...

> *To the united nation belong our external and mutual relations; to each State, severally, the care of our persons, our property, our reputation and religious freedom.*[17]

Jefferson understood clearly that the First Amendment ban on establishing religion only applied to the Congress and the federal government.

...taking from the States the moral rule of their citizens, and subordinating it to the general authority [federal government]...would break up the foundations of the Union[18]....I believe the States can best govern our home concerns, and the general [federal] government our foreign ones.[19]

Jefferson issued a warning and expressed concerns for the future "if the moral rule of the citizens of States were transferred to the federal government." The U.S. Supreme Court started the process in *Roe v. Wade (1973)* and in *Lawrence v. Texas (2003)*. In those decisions the Court struck down as unconstitutional some long standing laws of States. Those laws had banned the killing of babies in their mothers' wombs (abortion) and criminalized the moral perversion of sodomy. Both decisions used the 14th Amendment right to due process as the basis for their "right of privacy" decisions. Justice Thomas, in his dissent in the *Lawrence v. Texas* sodomy decision, pointed out that a "right to privacy" cannot be found in the Bill of Rights or any other part of the Constitution. Those in the 39th Congress who wrote the 14th Amendment and the States which ratified it would have been shocked and appalled at any suggestion that what they did would result in the legalization of sodomy.

Thomas Jefferson feared that unbridled federal courts would tear down "the wall of separation" the founders built into the Constitution. The founders goal was protecting the States from what they feared could become an all-powerful and oppressive federal government. The founders added the 9th and 10th Amendments to strengthen the wall of protection they believed the Constitution had already created. The Tenth Amendment has been, in effect, almost abolished by the Supreme Court thorough its incorporation of the Bill of Rights into the Fourteenth Amendment.

Again and again in his letters and in his autobiography, Jefferson spelled out clearly and succinctly the founders belief that...

...the States can best govern home concerns, and the General Government our foreign ones.[20]...The true theory of our Constitution is surely the wisest and best, that the States are independent as to everything within themselves, and united as to everything respecting foreign nations.[21]

Jefferson feared that breaking down that "wall of separation" between the States and the federal government would take the nation back to the oppressions of a strong central government. This fear motivated his writing the *Declaration of Independence* which resulted in the War for Independence. Jefferson wrote:

> *When all government, domestic and foreign, in little as in great things, shall be drawn to Washington as the center of all power, it will render powerless the checks provided of one government on another and will become as venal and oppressive as the government from which we separated.*[22]

The breakdown of the distinction between what was federal and what belonged to the States which Jefferson feared largely came to pass during the 20th Century.

To understand how it has been done requires a study and understanding of what has already been cited above:

(1) Why the original Bill of Rights was added to the Constitution and how and to whom it was meant to apply,

(2) Why the Fourteenth Amendment was written and adopted,

(3.) The meaning and basis for the concept of incorporation, and...

(4) How the Supreme Court's incorporation of the Bill of Rights into the 14th Amendment is the basis on which the Court prohibits prayer, reading of the Bible, posting of the Ten Commandments in schools. It is also the basis for overturning State jurisdiction over other key domestic areas such as matters of morality, schools, elections, courts and criminal justice systems, etc.

FEDERAL CONTROL OF CRIMINAL JUSTICE

Attacks on religious freedom and protection of basic morality by the States are not the only Supreme Court attacks on traditional freedoms and practices. Through *incorporation,* Supreme Court 14th Amendment decisions in the 1960s produced "a revolutionary change in the criminal process." Ultimate oversight and control of the criminal justice system was transferred from the States to the federal courts when the Supreme Court selectively incorporated the Bill of Rights including the Sixth Amendment right to counsel in criminal cases into the 14th Amendment.

Under Chief Justice Earl Warren the Court rewrote the criminal law and police procedures of the States starting with *Escobedo v. State of Illinois (1964)*. In *Miranda v. Arizona (1966),* the Warren Court went a step further in crippling state efforts to maintain justice and enforce the law. Anthony Lewis, normally a very liberal *New York Times* court observer, was quoted as saying that some considered that the Supreme Court was...

...trying to legislate a detailed criminal code for a continental country.[23]

A *New York Times* essay by Anthony Lewis on the change was headlined, "The Case That Changed America's Justice System."[24]

In his dissent in the Escobedo case, Justice Potter Stewart wrote that the overall result of the Court's decision...

...frustrates the vital interests of society in preserving the legitimate and proper function of honest and purposeful police investigation.[25]

The Sixth Amendment right to counsel in criminal cases was first applied to the States in *Gideon v. Wainwright (1963)*. In the Escobedo and Miranda decisions which followed, the Court not only applied the Sixth Amendment right to counsel to the States but went several steps further. It required that before law enforcement personnel could even start their questioning, a suspect must be apprised of his right to remain silent. The suspect must also be given an opportunity to have a lawyer present.

Application of those decisions have hindered traditional police methods of investigation. In at least one case, *Brewer v. Williams (1977)*, a confessed murderer of a little girl was set free.[26] The changes also gave the Supreme Court ultimate authority over imposition of the death penalty on various types of murderers.

FEDERAL CONTROL OF ELECTIONS

Supreme Court 14th Amendment *incorporation* decisions gave the federal courts control of state and national elections. It was done in violation of the clear expressed intent of the 39th Congress, which wrote and adopted the 14th Amendment.

Those in the 39th Congress made it clear in their debates that their action had nothing to do with schools, elections and voting.

Those debates were printed each day in the *Congressional Record.* They can be examined in good libraries today.

The 14th Amendment had nothing to do with voting. That was shown by the fact that the 39th Congress and the states which adopted the 14th had to go on to adopt the 15th to give former slaves the right to vote. The Supreme Court itself upheld that position that the 14th Amendment had nothing to do with voting rights. Shortly after passage of the 14th, a woman claimed that the Amendment gave her the right to vote. The Court, in *Minor v. Happersett (1874),* denied her claim. The ruling said...

> *...after the adoption of the fourteenth amendment, it was deemed necessary to adopt a fifteenth...If suffrage was one of the privileges and immunities [of the Fourteenth], why amend the Constitution to prevent its being denied on the basis of race.*[27]

The 15th Amendment gave former slaves the right to vote. That amendment would not have been necessary if the right to vote was included in the 14th as the Court now contends.

By the 1960s, however, the Supreme Court ignored the clear stated intent of the 39th Congress that the 14th Amendment had nothing to do with voting rights. The Court also ignored the earlier Supreme Court ruling which upheld that position. In *Baker v. Carr (1962),* the Court gave federal courts the authority to oversee how State legislatures, city councils, and school boards made reapportionment decisions. The Court ruled that all apportionment decisions had to be based on the one man, one vote concept. The decision ruled unconstitutional the practice of many states of having one house of the state legislature apportioned geographically (with one legislator, for example, for each county while the other body would be based on population). Additional court decisions in the years that followed required apportionment decisions to be made so that blacks could be elected even if it required gerrymandering. Paul Kauper in *Some Comments of the Reapportionment Cases* called the *Baker v. Carr* decision "a new chapter in judicial adventurism." In his book, *Government By Judiciary,* Raoul Berger commented...

> *...Reapportionment may have been "wise," but did it represent the kind of emergency situation that at best arguably excuses judicial revision?....Reapportionment of state and local legislatures was*

not among the more pressing problems in post-World War II America.[28]

The reapportionment decisions have ultimately given the federal courts oversight over all sorts of election and voting questions. By the year 2000, the federal government and its courts were getting involved in voting issues including how long polls should stay open, whether voters could vote for a number of days or weeks in advance, what kinds of voting machines would be used, and how votes should be counted. These were and should be issues the States decide.

COURT ORDERED SCHOOL DESEGREGATION

Another *incorporation* decision which breached the "wall of separation" between the States and the federal government resulted in school desegregation. *Brown v. Board of Education (1954)* struck down *Plessey v. Ferguson (1896),* the Supreme Court decision which permitted separate but equal segregated schools.

The Supreme Court sought a just result in using the 14th Amendment to desegregate schools. However, the Court violated the clear intent and purpose of the 39th Congress which adopted the Amendment. That raises this question:

Is it ever right to do wrong to get a chance to do right?

Raoul Berger, during his career as a Harvard law school professor and New Deal bureaucrat, was a dedicated liberal. He was a strong opponent of both segregation and *incorporation*. In the chapter on school segregation in his book *Government By Judiciary*, Berger tried to put the Court's decision into perspective. He wrote:

> The "desegregation decision in Brown v. Board of Education was, as Richard Kluger called it, an act of "Simple Justice." It was a long overdue attempt to rectify the grievous wrongs done to the blacks. For the legal historian, however, the question is whether the Fourteenth Amendment authorized the Supreme Court to perform that act. For the Court, like every agency of government, may act only within the limits of its constitutional powers.*[29]

Berger then quotes extensively from the *Congressional Record*. Those in the 39th Congress who wrote and adopted the 14th Amendment clearly specified in their debates that the Amendment in no way dealt with school segregation. Berger added:

Commentary of the Court's decisions frequently turns on whether they harmonize with the commentators own predilections. My study may be absolved of that imputation. I regard segregation as a blot on our society.[30]

Even so, Berger compiled a devastating assortment of evidence from the 39th Congress itself and the more current writings of those like himself who wanted to abolish segregation. That evidence shows that desegregation should not have been done through the Fourteenth Amendment. Most impressively, Berger's book quoted the memorandum prepared by Justice Felix Frankfurter's brilliant law clerk Alexander Bickel. Bickel summarized the research he did for Frankfurter for the desegregation case. Concerning segregation and the 14th Amendment, Bickel's memorandum said:

It is impossible to conclude that the 39th Congress intended that segregation be abolished; it is impossible also to conclude that they foresaw it might be, under the language they were adopting....there is no evidence whatever showing that for its sponsors the civil rights formula had anything to do with unsegregated schools. Wilson, [the Fourteenth Amendment] sponsor in the House, specifically disclaimed any such notion.[31]

Frankfurter had Bickel's research printed and distributed to every member of the Court. Then, without precedents or a Constitutional basis for the decision, the Court unanimously approved Chief Justice Earl Warren's decision in *Brown v. Board of Education*. The decision overturned *Plessey v. Ferguson*, the 1896 decision which permitted separate but equal schools. The desegregation decision was pure sociological jurisprudence, based, not on precedents or the Constitution, but on psychological and sociological studies, including Swedish socialist Gunnar Myrdal's 1944 book, *An American Dilemma*. Warren's decision said:

In approaching this problem, we cannot turn the clock back to 1868 when the Amendment was written, or even to 1896 when Plessey v. Ferguson was written.[32]

Berger in his book commented that this statement was...

...a veiled declaration that the intention of the founders was irrelevant and that the Court was revising the Constitution to meet present day needs.[33]

Warren's decision was one of a number of on-going decisions which ignore precedents. The decisions create the new "Living Constitution" through judge-made law. The approach has converted the Supreme Court into a continuing Constitutional Convention. Even though this method might more quickly solve what appears to be a pressing national problem, Berger says that such an approach is neither right—nor necessary. The founders had created a way to deal with school segregation and other problems which develop in "a changing world." What they intended was the amendment procedure spelled out in Article V of the Constitution.

Thirty years before *Brown v. Board of Education,* the nation had used the constitutional way to achieve justice for women. Under the laws of most States, women had no right to vote. To achieve justice and give women the right to vote, the Congress and the States passed the 19th Amendment. If the problem had existed in the 1950s, a five member majority of the Supreme Court would likely have used the 14th Amendment approach. The Court could have simply decreed that women had a constitutional right to vote.

For the nation's first 160 years, jurisdiction over "domestic matters" were reserved to themselves by the States when they wrote and adopted the Constitution. Their intent was made even more clear when the "wall of separation" between the States and Washington was strengthened through adoption of the 9th and 10th Amendments.

That "wall of separation" has been breached. Supreme Court decisions have almost eliminated the "wall of separation.".

DID CHANGES RESULT IN 9-11 ATTACKS?

The appointment of Earl Warren as Chief Justice of the United States was to have an impact in destroying the security laws of the United States not fully felt for several years. In the three year, 1956-58 period, the Supreme Court decided 52 cases involving communism and subversion in government. The decisions supported the Communist position 41 times, the anti-Communist position only 11 times. Under Warren's leadership, the Court used the Fourteenth Amendment *incorporation* process to void the long-standing anti-sedition laws of 42 states. Communists convicted under them were freed.[34] The government was denied the right to fire federal employees who were proved to have contributed money and services to Communist organizations.[35]

Schools and colleges were denied the right to fire teachers who refused to answer questions about their Communist activities.[36]

Because of the restrictions the Supreme Court, under Earl Warren, placed on investigation of communists and their activities by the States and various federal security agencies and the investigating committees of Congress, slowed down in the 1960s and almost halted in the mid-1970s. The on-going restrictions hindered federal and state investigations which could have uncovered the 9/11 plot before the tragedies happened.

Apologists for the Supreme Court's decisions justified them as "leaning over backwards to protect the rights of the individual." However, when the *individual* was a Yugoslavian *anti-Communist* refugee, the Court denied his right to political asylum. Andrew Artukovic, who lived with his wife and children in California, was forced to submit to an extradition hearing based on political charges made by the Communist government of Yugoslavia.[37]

The New York *Daily News*, then the largest circulation newspaper in America, even suggested impeachment of justices whose decisions consistently favored the Communists.[38]

All sorts of stop-gap corrective measures including Band-Aid type Constitutional Amendments have been proposed to reverse or correct what the Court has done. Few will work or ever be adopted.

Congress does have a constitutional remedy. The remedy is used regularly when a powerful legislator wants to keep the Courts from interfering with a pet project. It has rarely been used in dealing with real problems. Article III, Sections 1 and 2 of the Constitution establishes the U.S Supreme Court and its jurisdiction. Congress is given the authority to establish lesser courts. The Constitution gives the Congress the power to define the areas in which such Courts can operate. The Congress, for example, could limit the authority of federal courts to involve themselves in issues such as abortion, matters involving prayer and the public acknowledgement of God and any other issues over which the Congress by majority vote wanted to limit the authority of the Courts. In 2004, for example, the House of Representatives by an overwhelming vote denied courts the right to intervene in cases involving the mention of God in the Pledge of Allegiance to the flag. To be effective the measure would also have to be passed by the Senate.

Senator Tom Daschle of South Dakota when he was the Senate Minority leader had a provision inserted into an environmental bill that said that federal courts had no jurisdiction over whether or not South Dakota farmers could burn brush in clearing areas for farming. The Constitution allows the Congress to use the procedure to limit the jurisdiction of the lower federal courts over areas. The action would keep such issues from ever getting to the Supreme Court which is only given appellate jurisdiction by the Constitution

Correcting problems can't happen unless and until concerned citizens come to understand the Biblical foundations of American freedom and government. Those foundations produced the structure on which the United States grew great and strong. With an understanding of those foundations, individual Americans can and must commit themselves to returning America to again being "One Nation Under God."

CHAPTER IX

CAN THE STATE ACKNOWLEDGE GOD OR IS IT UNCONSTITUTIONAL?

The wicked shall be turned into hell, and all nations that forget God.

—*Psalms 9:17*

ANTI-GOD, ANTI-MORALITY COURT DECISIONS since 1962 have concerned many Americans and outraged others. These decisions of the U.S. Supreme Court as mentioned earlier include:

Banning of prayer and Bible reading in America's schools, forbidding the posting of the Ten Commandments in public buildings and the legalization of abortion and sodomy.

Lower courts have followed the lead of the Supreme Court. They have also handed down too many anti-God, anti-morality decisions to count. Some already mentioned warrant repeating. They include:

Jennifer Coffman, a Clinton-appointed federal judge, banned public display of the Declaration of Independence. She also banned display of the national motto, In God We Trust. Excerpts from other official and historical documents including the Constitution of the state of Kentucky were also banned. She justified her order because each of these founding documents mentioned God. She ruled that such mentions of God violated what she called the "wall of separation between church and state."[1]

...the 3rd Circuit Federal Appeals Court ruled that an Egg Harbor, New Jersey school district was correct constitutionally. It stopped a kindergarten student from distributing pencils which said, "Jesus Loves Little Children" to classmates at a holiday party at school.[2]

...the 9th Circuit Court of Appeals in California in 2003 declared that saying the words "under God" in the pledge to the flag by school children was unconstitutional.[3]

Other widespread restrictions on the public acknowledgement of God have affected every area of society. Scared school administrators, other public officials and even private employers implemented their own restrictions on demonstrations of faith and public acknowledgement of God. (Though none appear to include banning the use of His Name in cursing.) Through such restrictions, officials apparently hoped to avoid harassment and the costs of lawsuits filed by the American Civil Liberties Union (ACLU) and its followers.

As a result, the nation may eventually be in danger of either forgetting God—or denying Him.

The foundation for limiting the acknowledgement of God was laid in 1947 in the Supreme Court's decision in *Everson v. Board of Education*.[4] That decision itself was not particularly hostile to religion. In fact, the decision allowed New Jersey to provide funds for transporting children to Catholic and other private schools. However, Justice Hugo Black's decision in the case mentioned a "wall of separation between church and state." The decision, however, seemed to indicate that the mentioned "wall of separation" didn't apply in that case.

Since then, the phrase has been applied again and again in court decisions which limit the public acknowledgement of God. As a result, too many Americans today think the phrase "wall of separation between church and state" is in the Constitution. Those words are not there.

The real flood of anti-God, anti-morality decisions started in 1962 when the Supreme Court banned prayer in schools. In *Engel v. Vitale* the Court, without any precedents, ruled that the reciting of a non-denominational prayer in New York schools was unconstitutional. The prayer said:

> *Almighty God, we acknowledge our dependence upon Thee, and we beg Thy blessings upon us, our parents, our teachers, and on our Country.*[5]

In ruling that prayer unconstitutional, the U.S. Supreme Court ignored the opinions of distinguished judges and the rulings of lower courts which had considered the case. David Limbaugh in his excellent book, *Persecution—How Liberals Are Waging War Against Christianity*,[6] quoted First Amendment scholar George Goldberg who said:

*Of the first thirteen judges who considered the constitutionality
of the Regent's Prayer, among whom were some of the most
learned appellate judges in the nation, eleven found it valid, a
batting average of .846; and some of them felt strongly that any
other decision would be historically wrong and itself constitutionally objectionable.*[7]

The chief judge of the New York Court of Appeals said:

*Not only is this prayer not a violation of the First Amend-
ment...but holding that it is such a violation would be in defiance
of all American history, and such a holding would destroy a part
of the essential foundation of the American governmental structure.*[8]

One of the concurring Court of Appeals judges was even stronger.
He said:

*It is not mere neutrality to prevent voluntary prayer to a Creator;
it is an interference by the courts, contrary to the plain language
of the Constitution, on the side of those who oppose religion.*[9]

The Engel ruling against prayer in New York schools was the first
of an on-going series of openly anti-God, anti-Bible, anti-morality
Supreme Court decisions. The following year, a Unitarian couple
protested the reading of the Bible in Pennsylvania schools. Their
case, *School District of Abington Township v. Schempp,*[10] was joined
with a similar one from Maryland filed by renowned atheist
Madalyn Murray. In its decision, the Supreme Court ruled that long
standing Pennsylvania and Maryland state laws which required
each school day to open with Bible reading and prayer were unconstitutional. The Supreme Court's 61-page decision in *Abington
Township v. Schempp* included this statement:

*Because of the prohibition of the First Amendment against the
enactment by Congress of any law "respecting an establishment
of religion," <u>which is made applicable to the States by the Fourteenth Amendment,</u> no state law or school board may require that
passages from the Bible be read or that the Lord's Prayer be recited
in the public schools of a State at the beginning of each school
day—even if individual students may be excused from attending
or participating in such exercises...*[11] *(Emphasis added.)*

Until the Court made its decisions in the Engel and Abington cases, over thirty states either required or permitted prayer and Bible reading in schools. (As implemented in the Pennsylvania school where the author grew up, the law had each school day opened with the reading of ten verses of Old Testament scripture, prayer, the pledge to the flag and the singing of a Christian or patriotic hymn.) It had been done during the previous 160 years since Congress and the States added the First Amendment to the Constitution.

The Abington case continues to provoke discussion and criticism. A 1995 prize-winning essay by Cale L. Corbett opened with the statement:

> *In February 1963, the Supreme Court of the United States heard a First Amendment case which would forever change the way Americans viewed the Court and the value given religion by the highest magistrate in the land. In fact, this case is vilified as one that "kicked God and prayer out of schools."*[12]

In his 73-page concurrence to *Torcaso v. Watkins—1961,*[13] (which was another significant First Amendment case) Justice William Brennan made two landmark statements. They indicate the shifting judicial philosophy of the Court. Anticipating the Abington case which the high court would not consider for almost two years, Brennan wrote:

> *The Baltimore and Abington schools offend the First Amendment because they sufficiently threaten in our day those substantive evils the fear of which called forth the Establishment Clause....Our interpretation of the First Amendment must necessarily be responsive to the much more highly charged nature of religious questions in contemporary society. A too literal quest for the advice of the Founding Fathers upon the issues of these cases seems to me futile and misdirected.*[14] *(Emphasis added.)*

Brennan's remarks point up the Supreme Court tendency to ignore the original intent behind the writing and enactment of the Constitution. His statement also shows the Court's tendency to base decisions on the changing views of contemporary society. Decisions should be based on the absolute truth from which law was once derived. Brennan's comments indirectly acknowledge that the First

Amendment would never have been interpreted at the time of its writing to prohibit prayer and Bible reading in schools.

The words of Joseph Story should give insights into the true meaning and goal of the First Amendment. Story, as shown earlier, was appointed to the U.S. Supreme Court by President James Madison (acknowledged as the author of the First Amendment.) Story was the youngest man ever appointed to the Supreme Court. He served for 34 years. While serving those years on the Court, Story was also a professor at Harvard Law School. His writings on law and the Court are tremendously influential. In *A Familiar Exposition of the Constitution of the United States,* published in 1840, Story wrote this understanding of the First Amendment:

> *We are not to attribute this prohibition of a national religious establishment to an indifference to religion in general, and especially to Christianity (which none could hold in more reverence than the framers of the Constitution)....*
>
> *Probably, at the time of the adoption of the Constitution, and of the Amendment to it now under consideration, the general, if not the universal, sentiment in America was, that Christianity ought to receive encouragement from the State so far as it was not incompatible with the private rights of conscience and the freedom of religious worship.*
>
> *Any attempt to level all religions, and to make it as matter of state policy to hold all in utter indifference, would have created universal disapprobation, if not universal indignation.*[15]

In his commentary on the First Amendment's original meaning, Justice Joseph Story wrote:

> *The real object of the First Amendment was not to countenance, much less advance Mohammedanism, or Judaism, or infidelity, by prostrating Christianity, but to exclude all rivalry among Christian sects [denominations] and to prevent any national ecclesiastical patronage of the national government.*[16]

The original intent of the founders and those who actually wrote the Constitution and the Bill of Rights are important. The judges who ruled Bible reading and prayer in school unconstitutional should consider Story's comments. Today's judges, educators and media commentators should do likewise.

After Engel and Abington, the next landmark ruling banned posting of the Ten Commandments in schools. To give students an understanding of the basis of many laws, the Kentucky legislature passed a law allowing the Ten Commandments to be posted in Kentucky school rooms. The commandments are the basis of laws against murder, stealing, immorality, etc. Private funds paid for posting the Commandments in classrooms. The bottom of each poster carried the legislature's reason for permitting the posting of the commandments in the classroom. The explanation said:

> *The secular application of the Ten Commandments is clearly seen in its adoption as the fundamental legal code of Western Civilization and the Common Law of the United States.*[17]

The U.S. Supreme Court in *Stone v. Graham* ruled that such use of the Ten Commandments in the classroom was unconstitutional. The Court said the Ten Commandments had to go because:

> *The preeminent purpose for posting the Ten Commandments on schoolroom walls is plainly religious in nature. The Ten Commandments are undeniably a sacred text in the Jewish and Christian faiths, and no legislative recitation of a supposed secular purpose can blind us to that fact.*[18]

The Court's decision added this reason for declaring the posting of the Ten Commandments unconstitutional:

> *If the posted copies of the Ten Commandments are to have any effect at all, it will be to induce the school children to read, meditate upon, and perhaps venerate and obey, the Commandments.*[19]

The Court's decision said that this...

> *...is not a permissible state objective under the Establishment Clause.*[20]

How would today's Supreme Court respond to the words of James Madison, the fourth president of the United States and the principal author of the U.S. Constitution? Madison said:

> *We have staked the whole future of American civilization not upon the power of government, far from it. We have staked the future of our political institutions upon the capacity of mankind for self-government; upon the capacity of each and all of us to govern-*

ment ourselves, to control ourselves, to sustain ourselves according to the Ten Commandments of God.[21]

Statements such as Madison's and those of other founders, our founding documents and previous Supreme Court rulings provided the basis for the U.S. Supreme Court 1892 decision in *Church of the Holy Trinity v. U.S.* The Supreme Court decision in this landmark case described the United States as a "Christian nation," saying:

> *This is historically true. From the discovery of this continent to the present hour, there is a single voice making this affirmation....These are not individual sayings, declarations of private persons: they are organic utterances; they speak the voice of the entire people....These and many other matters which might be noticed, add a volume of unofficial declarations to the mass of organic utterances that <u>this is a Christian nation.</u>*[22] *(Emphasis added.)*

Even so, the anti-God, anti-prayer anti-Bible decisions have continued to come from the Supreme Court. Lower court decisions have followed the Supreme Court rulings. Prominent among them are two which effectively struck down school authority to permit prayer at high school graduations and athletic events. Those decisions include:

> *In Lee v. Weisman - 1992, the U. S. Supreme Court held that prayer at graduation was school sponsored when selected clergy were provided a pamphlet setting forth non-sectarian prayer guidelines.*[23]

> *In Santa Fe Independent School District v. Doe - 2000, the U. S. Supreme Court ruled that the school district was unconstitutionally endorsing religion when it allowed students to vote on whether to have prayer before games. Students who voted to have prayer would select who would give the prayer.*[24]

What's really behind the on-going court decisions which ban prayer and Bible reading, posting of the Ten Commandments, etc.? The ultimate goal of such decisions appears to be banning any public acknowledgement of God in society. The first open indication of that showed up in the Kentucky decision of a federal court cited earlier.

> *Jennifer Coffman, a Clinton-appointed federal judge, banned public display of the Declaration of Independence, the national*

motto, In God We Trust, and excerpts from other official and historical documents including the Constitution of the state of Kentucky. She justified her order because each of these founding documents mentioned God.[25]

The U.S. Supreme Court by a 5 to 4 vote on June 27, 2005 upheld Judge Coffman's ruling banning display of the Declaration of Independence and other historic documents mentioning God. Justice David Souter's rambling and sometimes inconsistent 24-page decision not only ignored the pro-God position and statements of the Founders, he denied them. Souter's opinion in *McCreary County of Kentucky et al. v. ACLU et al.* said:

> *...there is also evidence supporting the proposition that the Framers intended the Establishment Clause to require governmental neutrality in matters of religion, including neutrality in statements acknowledging religion.*[26]

Souter and the justices who supported him were not ignorant. Justice Antonin Scalia's 25-page dissent gave them the long history of public support for religion by the Founders. Quote after quote from the Founders showed the vital need for religion and Christianity for maintaining a free nation and government. Early chapters of this book presented the same quotes. Justices who made the Court's 5-4 decision denied the history. Scalia's dissent asked:

> *With all of this reality (and much more) staring it in the face, how can the Court possibly assert that "the First Amendment mandates governmental neutrality between religion and nonreligion."*
>
> *Nothing stands behind the Court's assertion that governmental affirmation of the society's belief in God is unconstitutional except the Court's own say so, citing as support only the unsubstantiated say-so of earlier Courts going back no farther than the mid-20th century.*[27]

Scalia characterized the Ten Commandments decision as illustrating "the dictatorship of a shifting Supreme Court majority."

That any public acknowledgement of God is considered by the Supreme Court to be an unconstitutional violation of the First Amendment became obvious in 2003. Alabama Chief Justice Roy Moore became known as the Ten Commandments judge. He was removed from the office to which the voters of Alabama had elected him. Most Americans have the impression that he was removed from office because he violated the First Amendment to the U.S. Constitution. Moore had installed a monument displaying the Ten Commandments in the lobby of the Alabama State Judicial Building. However, that is not why Roy Moore was removed from office.

The more than 220 pages of court decisions and transcripts in the case show that Judge Moore's "crime" was not the installation of the Ten Commandments monument. Moore's "crime" was his insistence that their placement acknowledged that God was God and that He is sovereign over the affairs of men and their governments.

A federal court judge, Myron Thompson, in ordering the removal of the monument said:

> ...in announcing this holding today, the court believes it is important to clarify at the outset that the court does not hold that it is improper in all instances to display the Ten Commandments in government buildings.[28]

Why then did the Judge Thompson order the removal of the Ten Commandment monument from the Alabama judicial building? In his 78-page order, Thompson details why. He states that he evaluated (1) Moore's Christian testimony, (2) the fact that Moore had run for office as "The Ten Commandments Judge," (3) speeches Moore made, and (4) some TV programs Dr. D. James Kennedy of Coral Ridge Ministries had run. The TV programs approved Moore's display of the Ten Commandments. Judge Thompson said additionally:

> The Chief Justice sent a thank-you note to campaign contributors reading, in part, "It is our hope that next year at this time, the Ten Commandments will be displayed in the Alabama Supreme Court, and the acknowledgement of God will be permitted and encouraged in all Alabama public forums under then Chief Justice Moore's leadership."[29]

Thompson concluded that Moore's *purpose* in displaying the Ten Commandments with other historic documents in the judicial building was not historical or secular but religious. In that Moore's *purpose* was an acknowledgement of God, the judge ruled that his action was *an unconstitutional establishment of religion.*

In that Moore was being charged with *an unconstitutional establishment of religion,* Moore and his attorneys asked the Court to define *religion.* At his trial and in a law review article Judge Moore had defined religion as understood at the time of the founding. His definition agreed with that found in *Noah Webster's 1828 Dictionary.* That definition said that *religion* means nothing more than...

> *...the duties we owe to our Creator and the manner of discharging those duties.*[30]

That was the standard in early America. On the basis of that definition of *religion,* Congress was prohibited from defining (or establishing) what duties we owe to our Creator and how they were to be carried out. Moore contended that definition and common sense indicate that displaying a Ten Commandment monument certainly falls short of *an establishment of religion.* That was the "crime" with which Moore was charged. When Judge Thompson rejected Moore's definition of religion, Moore and his attorneys asked Thompson to define *religion.* The Judge refused. In his order Thompson wrote:

> *...the court lacks the expertise to formulate its own definition of religion for First Amendment purposes. Therefore, because the court cannot agree with the Chief Justice's definition of religion and cannot formulate its own, it must refuse the Chief Justice's invitation to define "religion."*[31]

In effect, Judge Moore was being charged with a violation or "crime" which the court would not or could not define for him. The author is not an attorney. However, the Court's refusal to define the crime with which he was charged would appear to be a violation of Judge Moore's constitutionally protected *right to due process.*

Judge Thompson refused to accept Judge Moore's definition of religion (which was the accepted definition when the First Amendment was written). The federal judge explained that if Moore's definition were accepted, all sorts of Supreme Court First Amendment cases banning school prayers, Bible reading, and other religious displays or acknowledgements, would have to be decided differently. That extraordinary admission was written into the judge's ruling.[32]

Judge Roy Moore's "crime" was his public recognition of God. That became even more obvious when he was "tried" by the Alabama Court of the Judiciary. He was charged with violating the Canons of Judicial Ethics when he refused to accept Judge Thompson's orders. At the close of the hearing before the nine-member body of judges, Alabama Attorney General William Pryor who prosecuted the case questioned Moore. On the video which recorded the proceeding, Pryor addressed Moore and said:

Your understanding here is that the federal court ordered that you could not acknowledge God. Is that correct? [33]

Moore answered, "Yes." Pryor continued the questioning.

And if you resume your duties as Chief Justice after this proceeding, you will continue to acknowledge God as you have testified today you would, no matter what any official would say? [34]

Moore replied:

"Absolutely. Without—let me clarify that. Without an acknowledgement of God I cannot do my duties. I must acknowledge God. It says so in the Constitution of Alabama. It says so in the First Amendment of the United States Constitution. In says so in everything I've read." [35]

Attorney General Pryor continued:

The only point I'm trying to clarify, Mr. Chief Justice, it's not why, but only that in fact, if you do resume your duties as Chief Justice you will continue to do that without regard to what any other official says, Isn't that right? [36]

Moore replied:

Well, I'll do the same thing this court did in starting with prayer. That's an acknowledgement of God. I would do the same thing that justices do when they place their hand on the Bible and say, "So help me God." It's an acknowledgement of God. The Alabama Supreme Court opens with "God save the State and this Honorable court." It's an acknowledgement of God. In my opinions—I've written many opinions—acknowledging God is the source, the moral source of our law. [37]

After hearing Judge Moore indicate that he would continue to acknowledge God in performing his duties, the Alabama Court of the Judiciary ruled:

> During the trial of this matter the Chief Justice maintains his defiance, testifying that he stood by an earlier statement given by him to the judicial inquiries commission in which he stated in part, "I did what I did because I upheld my oath and that's what I did. So, I have no apologies for it. I would do it again." The Chief Justice shows no contrition for his actions. Because of the magnitude of the decision with regard to sanctions for the Chief Justice's violation of the Canons of Judicial Ethics it was a difficult one for this court to make. Finding no other viable alternative, this court hereby orders that Roy S. Moore be removed from his position as Chief Justice of the Supreme Court of Alabama. This court is now adjourned.[38]

In a later speech in Branson, Missouri Judge Moore said:

> The issue in Alabama was not about the Ten Commandments or a monument. The issue was not about religion. The issue was whether or not the state can acknowledge God.[39]

That Judge Moore's judgment is true was shown by what happened after he was removed from the Alabama Supreme Court. After Moore's dismissal, the remaining justices placed their own Ten Commandments display in the Supreme Court chambers. Their display included the Commandments, the Magna Charta, the *Declaration of Independence* and other documents from history.

Why is this new display legal and Judge Moore's monument was not? The purpose of Judge Moore's monument was acknowledging the sovereignty of God. Moore's monument was moved into a closet. The new display is made up of what are considered to be historical artifacts which are displayed where man is in control. As long as the display is not acknowledging God, the display is just history. That the judges say is OK.

In Psalm 9:17, God says:

> The wicked shall be turned into hell, and all nations that forget God.

CHAPTER X

WILL MEN AGAIN PLEDGE THEIR LIVES, FORTUNES, AND SACRED HONOR?

...whenever any Form of Government becomes destructive of these Ends, it is the right of the people to alter or abolish it, and to institute new Government, laying its Foundation on such principles, and organizing its Powers in such Form, as to them shall seem most likely to effect their Safety and Happiness. Prudence, indeed, will dictate that Governments long established should not be changed for light and transient Causes; and accordingly all Experience has shewn, that Mankind are more disposed to suffer, while Evils are sufferable, than to right themselves by abolishing the Forms to which they are accustomed.

—Declaration of Independence

JUDGE ROY MOORE IS THE BEST KNOWN of those who have lost public positions for acknowledging God. Gregory Thompson is another. Thompson was the superintendent of a small public school district in western Missouri. He had served there with distinction for over half a dozen years. His accomplishments had been acknowledged and recognized by his school board and the people in the community. His fellow southwest Missouri school superintendents elected him to head their regional school administrators association.

In August 2004 he was fired as superintendent of the Humansville, Missouri R-IV School District. His crime? Thompson refused to agree to the settlement of a lawsuit filed against him. He had been sued for acknowledging God in various ways in school activities. The settlement would have required him to never acknowledge God in the performance of his duties as the school superintendent. He said, "I can't do that."

The lawsuit was filed in federal court by the mother of a student in the school. The suit charged that Thompson, two other school district administrators and the seven members of the school board had engaged in acts which violated the separation of church and State. Their establishment of religion acts included:

Prior to the filing of the suit a plaque containing a version of the Ten Commandments had been displayed in the premises and property of the school district. The suit charged that Thompson had authorized the display because he believes Matthew 22:37-38 which says: "You shall love the Lord thy God with all your heart, and with all your soul, and with all your mind."[1]

The small Ten Commandments plaque had been displayed in the school for at least nine years. The plaque had been displayed for three years before Thompson came to Humansville as superintendent. In addition to having the Commandments posted, the suit charged that:

Public meetings of the school board opened with prayer. Recitation of prayers was permitted at school activities and events including Veterans' Day assemblies and athletic banquets. Prayer meetings were held on school premises before school started on Wednesday mornings. They were attended by students, teachers, parents, and local pastors.[2]

The suit charged that these prayer meetings constituted an "an endorsement of religion." After the suit was filed, the posted Ten Commandments plaque "disappeared." However, several days later almost the entire high school student body came to school wearing T-shirts with the Ten Commandments on them. The law suit said that when Thompson publicly stated that the students action was...

"...a beautiful response from the children," it was an endorsement of religion by him.[3]

The court complaint also charged Thompson with having in his office and on his desk...

...visible to students, parents, teachers, staff and members of the public...a Christian crucifix, a "praying hands" sculpture, and a Bible...each of which constitute an endorsement of the sectarian religious message of these symbols.[4]

Thompson's big "crime" according to the federal lawsuit was that he...

...displayed on his automobile, on school premises and visible to students, parents, teachers and staff of Humansville schools, a bumper sticker that read, "Keep the Ten Commandments." Such act, the suit said, reasonably conveys to viewers of this bumper

sticker an endorsement of the religious message displayed there-on.[5]

A second count of the lawsuit, asked damages from Thompson and other school administrators. The suit charged that the eleventh grade boy whose mother filed the lawsuit had been subjected to verbal harassment by fellow students. The suit asked damages because...

> ...*Defendants [Thompson and other administrators] knew of the harassment by fellow students...were deliberately indifferent....and failed to take immediate and appropriate corrective action to deter or prevent this harassment, or to discipline students who engaged in this harassment.*[6]

School districts carry insurance to defend lawsuits against the district and its employees. The attorneys for the insurance company negotiated an agreement to settle the lawsuit. The insurance company agreed to pay $45,000 to the mother who filed the suit on behalf of her son.[7] In addition to the payment, the settlement basically would have required the district and the defendants to refrain from any future acknowledgements of God.

Thompson refused to agree so the suit could not be settled. Thompson wanted the charges against him tried before a jury. If he had agreed to the broad terms of the proposed settlement, Thompson could not have continued to use the words, "God bless," in signing letters, notes to staff, etc. To avoid a trial before a jury, the attorneys agreed to drop Thompson from the suit and settled the suit against the other defendants. The other defendants—the school board and the other administrators—agreed to the proposal. The suit was settled and the $45,000 was paid.

At that point, the attorney for the insurance company notified the school district that Thompson's retention as Superintendent could result in denial of the school district's insurance coverage. Another involved attorney was told that if the Humansville insurance were canceled, that no other company would be likely to insure the district.[8]

Why were the insurance company and its attorneys so anxious to settle the suit? Why did they oppose giving the man who was supposedly their client his opportunity to go before a jury? The reasons were basically economic.

When such a First Amendment case goes to trial in federal court, the attorneys for the complaining party can get big bucks.[9] If the jury decides that the defendants in any way violated various past court decisions which restrict acknowledgement of God in public schools, the judge can award attorneys fees. (How judges award the American Civil Liberties Union millions of dollars in such suits is discussed in the next chapter.) The school district insurance company would have been liable. When a federal case goes to trial, those fees could total $150,000. Rather than risk such a loss, the insurance company quickly agreed to the $45,000 settlement.

In a letter to the school district and the defendants, the insurance attorney listed what he termed were the guidelines concerning religious expressions. The guidelines, the attorney said, had been issued by the U.S. Department of Education. Summed up, those guidelines, in effect, state that school officials have to act and live in school as if there is no God. The list includes:

1. Public school officials must remain neutral in the treatment of religion. Neutrality includes personal expression, verbal and non-verbal, by school officials while engaged in the course of their duties.[10]

"Neutrality" also prohibits school officials from...

...encouraging or leading students in religious activities or co-mingling with students who initiated such on their own. Neutrality also prohibits school officials from exhibiting the crucifix, the Bible, the Ten Commandments and other religious symbols....or permitting the Bible and other religious materials to be distributed to students even by outsiders on school property.[11]

The guidelines, however, do not appear to deal with whether teachers could curse or take the name of the Lord in vain in class or in the presence of students.

Thompson could not accept what he saw in the guidelines as a ban on the acknowledgement of God. The insurance company attorneys said the guidelines came from the U.S. Department of Education.

said the guidelines came from the U.S. Department of Education. The school board therefore faced the difficult choice of firing Thompson or losing its insurance coverage.

Before the decision was made, Thompson met with and addressed the school board. Thompson reviewed the good things board members acknowledged had been accomplished. He had headed the district for six years. In an eight-page statement, Thompson told the board:

In your hearts, I know that you have to know it is because God was such a part of my life and through His son Jesus I was able to do good things for the children [of this district]. I have never hidden it—praying everywhere for their goodness and that of their families. I will always openly acknowledge Him—but never force Him on those who are not ready to know Him. [13]

Thompson then quoted the insurance company representatives. They told him that their list of ways that God was not to be acknowledged was not exhaustive. In effect, they said that he could not acknowledge God in any way. He then added:

I would rather die than be under that type of slavery... [14]

He shared quotations from George Washington and Thomas Jefferson which acknowledged God. He also read a quote from Samuel Adams, one of the signers of the Declaration of Independence. Adams' quotation dealt with why the legislature must prevail over the judiciary. Adams said:

If the public are bound to yield obedience to laws to which they cannot give their approbation [support], they are slaves to those who make such laws and enforce them. [15]

Thompson followed that quotation by Samuel Adams with his own words. He said:

The overwhelming majority of the people in this nation are slaves to the judicial whims that are against God. [16]

Thompson then spelled out for the school board the three choices they faced. Their first was:

Choose to acknowledge God in all ways for the children we serve, because we truly love them. Let everyone know that we are sticking together because we love the children and want to make sure that

*wisdom and peace. Let people know that we have a wonderful
thing going on in Humansville because we put God first. Let
people know that the Ten Commandments will always be up in
Humansville because it is an acknowledgement of God and the
moral code that our nation started with. Let the people know that
we will look to improve our children's lives with the Bible as part
of our curriculum as it was from the beginning of our country. We
will chose to do right in God's eye and not man's.*[17]

The second choice logically followed the first. He asked the board
to make this decision:

*We wish to continue to have Mr. T. be the leader of our district,
knowing that he will have the Ten Commandments up, knowing
that he will have his cross up, knowing that he will have the Bible
on his desk, knowing that he will pray openly for the veterans and
all of our troops that are in harms way, knowing that he will pray
for our children and families openly at every special occasion,
knowing that he will continue to put "God Bless" on all his
correspondence, knowing that he never promotes Baptist,
Catholic, Methodist or any other doctrine but that he will always
acknowledge God, knowing that he will try to see that children
are taught the truth so they can be free, knowing that his love for
all of us is rooted in the teaching of Jesus and we want that for
our children, knowing that he intends to put a Bible curriculum
into our district and that he intends to fight in every way for our
children.*[18]

Thompson then spelled out a third choice for the board:

*Because the insurance company has threatened that they would
not insure another First Amendment issue with respect to the
Establishment Clause, and because it could possibly cost money
out of district reserves, we will have to ask Mr. T. to step down.*[19]

On August 24, 2004, the Humansville R-IV school board then
voted 6-1 to terminate Thompson's contract as superintendent. The
contract had two years and ten months to go. Thompson was given
two months termination pay.[20] He also received this glowing recommendation:

*In all phases of his job, Mr. Thompson has demonstrated his
professional ability as an administrator. He is a very dedicated
individual. His positive attitude towards any task is very con-*

tagious. He is fair in his judgments, listening to all sides before rendering his decisions. His consistency in dealing with students and parents is well respected throughout the community....Mr. Thompson would be an asset to any organization lucky enough to have the good fortune of his presence...personally and professionally, he is NUMBER ONE.[21]

The recommendation then added these words from a former school board member who wrote:

I can't begin to express my gratitude for everything you've done...You have brought so much to our district and I personally appreciated that you brought God into our school.[22]

An experienced school attorney indicates that much of what Thompson did could have been accomplished under present law. But he would have had to do it properly with sound legal counsel. Even so, school insurers might not have approved, for, even done properly, acknowledging God can provoke controversy.

Another Christian attorney involved as an adviser approved the proposed settlement. He recommended that Thompson should avoid the temptation to be a martyr. He suggested that he should agree to the settlement and refrain from any acknowledgement of God in his school activities. By doing this, Thompson could then achieve a positive influence in the community in his off-duty hours. The attorney's recommendation said:

I personally believe that Greg Thompson can serve the highest and best use of his time and career by continuing in his current position as Superintendent of Schools. In other words, continue to serve the children he truly loves and "cool-it" on religious activities at school during school time.

That may have been good legal advice in view of the condition of the Courts—and the country at this time. He added:

Greg might wish to be fired thinking that it is a matter of principle. But my thought is being a martyr only means you will be gone and out of sight in a short period of time and forgotten. Unless you are going to write a book or do a movie, I wouldn't do this personally.

Fortunately, the 56 men who signed the *Declaration of Independence* on July 4, 1776 didn't follow such advice. They pledged their lives, their fortunes and their sacred honor to advance the cause of independence.

Such a time may be coming again for courageous individuals. Courts (or insurance companies) will try to stop others from acknowledging God as Greg Thompson did. Then people will have to choose.

The Humansville School Board was made up of good people. If they had chosen to stand with Thompson, they may have lost their insurance. Federal marshals ultimately could have enforced the edicts of federal judges. A few brave principled people may have ended up in jail for refusing to obey the "law" of a federal judge.

However, the overwhelming majority of Americans want God acknowledged in school. They want the Ten Commandments posted. If the day should come when school boards and the people they represent decide to pledge their lives, their fortunes and their sacred honor to the cause, there wouldn't be enough room in jails to hold them all. And there wouldn't be enough federal marshals to put them there.

Such an event probably won't happen soon. It won't happen until enough Americans yield themselves to be used by the Lord. When they do, they can be used to bring a revival of the sort which transformed America in the years between about 1740 and 1775. That revival produced the men who pledged their lives, their fortunes and their sacred honor when they signed the *Declaration of Independence.*

If enough people should now agree to let God use them, He might be pleased to bring another nation changing revival. That could move Congress to use its power under Article III, Section 2 of the U.S. Constitution. Under that provision, Congress can tell the Courts that they have no jurisdiction over issues concerning the acknowledgement of God by public officials or anyone else.

What will you do? Where will you stand?

MILLIONS OF TAXPAYER DOLLARS FINANCE ACLU LAWSUITS WHICH BAN PUBLIC ACKNOWLEDGEMENT OF GOD

We have defended the right of individuals to have freedom of choice in marriage and partnerships and engage in polygamy.

Nadine Strossen, President
American Civil Liberties Union

NEARLY EVERY DECISION restricting the public acknowledgement of God in America has been promoted, advocated or sued for by the American Civil Liberties Union (ACLU). The ACLU has been involved repeatedly in getting federal judges to ban any public display of crosses, other religious symbols or Christmas displays, nativity scenes, or other public acknowledgements of God. The ACLU in its history has had a varied agenda. During the 1950s and 1960s the ACLU regularly opposed and struck down efforts designed to keep communists from key positions in government. The ACLU also won court cases to protect communists who were teaching in America's school and colleges. Today, the organization files suits claiming same-sex couples have a right to marry, adopt babies or be foster parents. ACLU suits have also opposed abstinence education as "religious."

Many American citizens become outraged when courts agree with ACLU demands that acknowledgements of God be banned. They would be even more outraged to learn that judges, since 1976, have awarded the ACLU and its attorneys millions of dollars for filing such cases.

The American Legion Magazine, in its February 2005 issue, turned a spotlight on cases in which the ACLU and its attorneys were awarded huge fees by federal judges. The ACLU was representing people who were "offended" when they had to see or be exposed to a Cross, the Ten Commandments, or other acknowledgements of God. The magazine said that the case of *Buono v. Norton...*

> *...illustrates the ACLU's fanaticism and disrespect for veterans, and it exposes the threat of further legal attacks on veterans' memorials by the ACLU or others.*[1]

The magazine article described the situation which produced the case. The article said that:

> *In 1934, a private citizen desiring to honor World War I veterans made a cross of two pieces of pipe. The cross was mounted on a rock outcrop in a remote, privately owned area in California's Mojave Desert. President Clinton, as one of his last acts as president, issued an executive order incorporating the area into the Mojave National Preserve.*[2]

The ACLU quickly filed a federal suit demanding that the Cross be removed. The federal judge in his order agreed. He awarded the ACLU over $40,000 for handling the case.[3]

Veterans protested. The area's Congressman, Jerry Lewis (R-Calif.), got Congress to approve special legislation authorizing the transfer of the one acre site of the Cross to a private owner. In exchange, the owner gave the government five acres of private ground. The ACLU, still unsatisfied asked the Ninth Circuit Federal Courts of Appeals to declare the land transfer unconstitutional. On a technicality, the Appeals Court, in late 2004, kept the case open. The ACLU legal fees were increased by the judge to $63,000.

The American Legion article detailed case after case where federal judges awarded outrageous attorneys fees to the ACLU. The group had filed the law suits for clients who were protesting against religious expressions or other so-called civil rights violations. In one such case, the ACLU and its associated attorneys from the People for the American Way and the Southern Poverty Law Center received $500,000. They were given this half a million dollars for their work in driving the Ten Commandments out of the courthouse of Alabama Chief Justice Roy Moore.[4] Other such cases include:[5]

> *Courts ordered the City of San Diego to pay the ACLU $940,000. The city had surrendered to an ACLU demand that it kick the Boy Scouts out of the City's Balboa Park.*

Portland, Oregon Public Schools were ordered to pay the ACLU $108,000. The ACLU brought the case on behalf of an atheist who objected to the Boy Scouts being allowed to recruit boys during non-class time.

A major danger has developed from federal judges awarding attorneys fees to the ACLU in such cases. Many smaller cities, school districts and their insurance companies now bow to any ACLU demands. Schools fear having to pay such exorbitant fees if they try to fight in court for what they believe to be their rights. The American Legion, in a well researched article, cited several such situations:[6]

The city council of Redlands, California reluctantly surrendered to the ACLU's demand that it change the city seal to remove a Cross. They agreed rather than risk having a judge order the city to pay big attorney fees to the ACLU.

On a similar basis, the Los Angeles County Board of Supervisors by a 3-2 vote surrendered to the ACLU's demand. The county seal had to be changed to remove a tiny cross in one panel representing the mission period of LA's history.

The Duluth, Minnesota city council voted 5-4 to agree with an ACLU demand to remove a Ten Commandments monument from public property. The city couldn't afford to pay its own legal costs of defending the monument and risk paying the ACLU attorneys fees as well.[7]

The American Legion article was written by Rees Lloyd, a longtime civil-rights attorney. He had been a staff attorney for the ACLU of Southern California for two years after graduating from law school in 1979. He is a past commander of the Banning, California American Legion post. His article resulted from the ACLU's efforts described above to ban the cross from a veteran's memorial.

Lloyd and the American Legion really went on the offensive in 2004. President George W. Bush's Department of Defense had caved in to settle a 1999 ACLU lawsuit. That suit demanded a ban on Department of Defense sponsorship of Boy Scout troops by military units worldwide. Participation in the Boy Scouts includes an oath which has the words, "On my honor, I will do my best to do my duty to God and my country." The ACLU claimed DoD sponsorship of a group which had such an oath violated the U.S. Constitution.

The *American Legion Magazine* article highlighted the issue with a headline asking, "Where is the outrage?"[8] The article detailed how the DoD caved in to the ACLU on the Boy Scout issue. A letter from the Legion's National Commander Thomas P. Cadmus to Defense Secretary Donald Rumsfeld asked:

> *Is there no one in Washington, D.C., at the highest levels of government that will stand up for Scouts, for Scouting and support this movement that has long been an institution of highest reputation in America? Where's the president? Where's his cabinet? Where's the Congress? What are the courts doing? Where is the outrage?*[8]

The ACLU war against the Boy Scouts broadened in March 2005. In a letter to the Boy Scouts of America...

> *...the ACLU vowed to take legal action against public schools and other tax-payer funded agencies that charter Scout troops. The ACLU letter claimed that such sponsorship violates the separation of church and state.*[9]

The ACLU action is based on its objection to the traditional Boy Scout oath. Boys pledge, "On my honor, I will do my best to do my duty to God and my country."

In response to the ACLU threat, Boy Scouts spokesman Greg Shields told the Baptist Press that to protect the schools, the Scouts were pulling charters from schools which have been sponsoring troops.[10]

How has the ACLU gotten the power to get taxpayer money to fight recognitions of God? A column written by Eagle Forum founder Phyllis Schlafly in 2004 had a headline which said: "ACLU Finds Pot of Gold at the Foot of the Cross."[11] Mrs. Schlafly explained that the process of awarding such large fees started with a little known 1976 federal law called the Civil Rights Attorney's Fees Awards Act. With that law (42 U.S. Code, Section 1988) Congress allows judges to award attorney fees to plaintiffs in civil rights cases brought against local governments. Congress passed the law because many believed attorneys were reluctant to help poor people get justice if their rights were abused by local government agencies. While the law was designed to help plaintiffs in civil rights cases, Mrs. Schlafly said...

> ...*the ACLU is using it for First Amendment cases, asserting that it is a civil right NOT to see a cross or the Ten Commandments. The financial lure created by this law is the engine that drives dozens of similar cases nationwide. Every state, county, city, public park or school that has a cross, a Ten Commandments monument, or recites the Pledge of Allegiance, has become a target for ACLU fund raising.*[12]

There are continual outrages. The ACLU sued Kentucky for a Ten Commandments display on its state capitol grounds. Taxpayers of the Bluegrass State had to pay the ACLU $121,500. Taxpayers in one Tennessee county had to pay the ACLU $50,000 for the same offense.[13] Between 1979 and 1999, ACLU's annual income grew from $3.9-million to over $45-million.[14]

In some of the cases, the ACLU represented plaintiffs who demanded that crosses, other religious symbols or the Ten Commandments be removed. The people claimed they were offended when they had to see a symbol which acknowledged God when they were driving by or visiting a public sight.

Apparently, however, anyone offended when exposed to ACLU-protected pornography doesn't have a basis for relief in federal court. The ACLU has been involved in almost every court decision striking down restrictions which limit distribution of pornography in America. The organization claims to be upholding the precious right of freedom of speech guaranteed by the First Amendment.

However, there are inconsistencies. The ACLU supports "free speech" and "academic freedom" so teachers can advocate, say or teach anything in the classroom. At the same time, the ACLU and its affiliates oppose giving students in the classroom the same right if they desire to question their professors. Students at New York's Columbia University had protested to the New York Civil Liberties Union that they were being bullied and silenced in classrooms by certain professors. The professors were vehemently anti-Israel and pro-Muslim. The students were denied the right to question or oppose such views in class.

After the students protested, the New York Civil Liberties Union wrote to Lee Bollinger, the president of Columbia University saying...

> ...*students can criticize professors in various ways outside the classroom. They can even advance such criticism in class if permitted by the professor to do so.*[15]

Who makes up this American Civil Liberties Union? During its history the ACLU has regularly defended communists, the distribution of pornography, and special rights for homosexuals while opposing the rights of citizens to acknowledge God in a variety of ways. Why?

Many true civil libertarians become involved in the ACLU at times. They have a sincere interest in protecting constitutional rights of all citizens. Rees Lloyd, author of the American Legion article, was one of them. However, to put the actions and the positions of the ACLU into a correct perspective one must examine its history and origin.

The ACLU was founded in 1920. The founding director was Roger Baldwin. In his 1935 college-reunion yearbook Baldwin said:

> *I have continued directing the unpopular fight for the rights of agitation as director of the American Civil Liberties Union. I seek the social ownership of property, the abolition of the propertied class and sole control of those who produce wealth. Communism is the goal.*[16]

Baldwin was not alone. Joining him on the founding board of the ACLU were Rev. Harry F. Ward, Louis Budenz, Elizabeth Gurley Flynn, and William Z. Foster. All were communists. Ward organized what became the first officially-designated communist front in America, The Methodist Federation for Social Action. Both Foster and Flynn later became heads of the Communist Party U.S.A. (CPUSA). Budenz, until he broke with communism thirty years later, served for years as the editor of *The Communist Daily Worker.*[17]

Baldwin was active in the ACLU until 1981. His two books were *Letters From Soviet Prisons* and *Liberty Under The Soviets.* In his books, Baldwin expressed support for the communist "experiment" in the Soviet Union and for the Russian dictators Lenin and Stalin.

In *Letters From Soviet Prisons* Baldwin said the Russian Revolution was...

> ...*the greatest and most daring experiment yet undertaken to recreate society in terms of human values....of incalculable value to the development of the world.*[18]

Baldwin demonstrated a double standard so typical of Marxist-Leninist morality. In his book, *Liberty Under The Soviets,* Baldwin defended Soviet oppression, saying...

> ...*Repressions in the Western Democracies are violations of professed constitutional liberties, and I condemn them. Such repressions in the Soviet Union are weapons of a struggle in the transition period to socialism.*[19]

Earl Browder, General Secretary of the CPUSA, acknowledged that the ACLU was "a transmission belt" for the Communist Party. His statement was published on page 26 of the September 7, 1939 *New York Times.*

Today the ACLU claims to have over 400,000 members and supporters. Powerful people have been involved. Supreme Court Justice Ruth Bader Ginsberg was the General Counsel of the ACLU from 1973 to 1980.[20] She served on the ACLU Board of Directors during most of that period. Before going on the Supreme Court, Ginsberg taught at various law schools including Columbia, Harvard and Stanford. Her book, *Sex Bias in the U.S. Code* advocates such feminist demands as assigning women to military combat duty, federal financing of comprehensive daycare and sex integration of the Boy and Girl Scouts.

The New Hampshire Civil Liberties Union published a list titled *ACLU's 100 Greatest Hits: Cases in which the ACLU played a major role.*[21] The list shows that ACLU work in the religious field almost always limits religious rights. Exceptions come when it works to uphold the right of Jehovah's Witness children to refuse to salute the flag. The ACLU has also defended the free speech rights of a priest who gives racist, anti-Semitic speeches. The ACLU also defends flag burning and pornography as "free speech."

The ACLU efforts have strengthened the "rights" of criminals at the expense of the victims of crime. Its efforts expanded welfare rolls by getting the Supreme Court to strike down a rule that denied welfare to children whose unmarried mothers lived with men in violation of rules. Over 500,000 were added to welfare roles. The ACLU also advocated and supported the Court's rule in *Lawrence v. Texas* which gave constitutional rights to the practice of sodomy.

What will be next? The American Legion article said. "If Congress does not act, nothing in the law will prevent making the ACLU precedent against the single cross at the Mojave Desert Veterans Memorial applicable to the Crosses and Stars of David in every national cemetery."[22]

What can be done?

The September 2003 *Phyllis Schlafly Report* had the headline, "Congress Should Stand Up and Be Counted." Mrs. Schlafly wrote:

> *Federal court decisions banning the Pledge of Allegiance and the Ten Commandments, and the possibility raised in Lawrence v. Texas that marriage may no longer be defined as the union of a man and a woman, show that the time has come to curb the Imperial Judiciary. We should not allow federal judges [encouraged by the ACLU] to overturn principles that are at the heart of the American character, culture, and Constitution.*[23]

Delegates at the American Legion's 2004 National Convention agreed. Resolution 326, written by Rees Lloyd, the author of the Legion's magazine article quoted earlier, calls on Congress to end judges' authority to award attorney fees in cases brought "to remove or destroy religious symbols."[24] Representative John Hostettler (R-IN) introduced H.R. 3609 to achieve this goal.[25] Whether the bill will be reintroduced in the 2005 session is yet to be seen. Any such measure will certainly be opposed by the ACLU and the trial attorneys.

Chapter XIII discusses other corrective actions. They should be studied by anyone really interested in seeing America return to a true Republican Constitutional government.

SHOULD SUPREME COURT JUSTICES EVER BASE DECISIONS ON RULINGS OF INTERNATIONAL TRIBUNALS?

Against the insidious wiles of foreign influence the jealousy of a free people ought to be constantly awake, since history and experience prove, that foreign influence is one of the most baneful foes of Republican government.

—-*George Washington, Farewell Address*

JUSTICES WHO SERVE on the U.S. Supreme Court take an oath to uphold the Constitution of the United Sates. The Court on which they serve is charged with deciding whether the laws, actions and rulings of U.S. governmental bodies and individuals are compatible with the U.S. Constitution. The Constitution is the ultimate authority.

That being so, how can an increasing number of Supreme Court Justices, who have taken an oath to uphold the U.S. Constitution, be basing their decisions on precedents and practices established by foreign courts? How can the Court and its members increasingly look to rulings and decisions of international courts and commissions in deciding cases when the U.S. Constitution should be the final authority? How can they look to such foreign precedents in deciding what the U.S. Constitution should mean?

Such betrayal should not occur. The *Declaration of Independence* was signed by 56 men in 1776 to set us free from such foreign influence and authority. These men represented the colonies who formed the United States.

Yet, more and more Supreme Court decisions are based on rulings and decisions of European or international courts. Among such landmark foreign-based decisions are:

In a 1999 death penalty case, Justice Stephen Breyer referenced decisions from Jamaica, India, Zimbabwe, and the European Court of Human Rights to justify his statement that a growing number of courts outside the United States have held that lengthy delays in administering a lawful death penalty renders the ultimate execution "inhuman, degrading or unusually cruel."[1]

Because of court imposed delays and repeated appeals some murderers stay on death row for up to twenty years before being executed. Would Justice Breyer (and the foreign authorities) favor fewer appeals and quicker executions? Or are he and his foreign "authorities" just against all executions? Another example of foreign influence:

In 2002 the Supreme Court ruled that mentally retarded people convicted of murder could not be given a death sentence. Justice John Paul Stevens in his opinion said that "within the world community, the imposition of the death penalty for crimes committed by mentally retarded offenders is overwhelmingly disapproved." He cited a legal brief from the European Union as an authority for the decision.[2]

The European Union, of course, opposes all executions. Turkey, for example, was forced to abolish the death penalty before even being considered for possible admittance to the European Union.

Concerning the ruling in the 2002 *Atkins v. Virginia* death penalty case, Justice Clarence Thomas objected to the decision being based on foreign precedents. He said:

While Congress as a legislature may wish to consider actions of other nations on any issue, this Court's jurisprudence should not impose foreign moods, fads, or fashions on America.[3]

The landmark *Lawrence v. Texas* decision legalized sodomy in the United States. It struck down the laws in thirteen states which banned sodomy. Justice Anthony Kennedy wrote the opinion for the majority. Kennedy supported the Court's ruling that individuals have a constitutional right to engage in sodomy by citing three "authorities." They include the 1967 Act of the British Parliament which decriminalized sodomy, the European Convention on Human Rights, and a 1981 European Court of Human Rights case. In his decision, written for the Court's majority, Kennedy summed up his looking to foreign authorities by saying:

The right the petitioners seek in this case [to engage in sodomy] has been accepted as an integral part of human freedom in many other countries....values we share with a wider civilization.[4]

Justice Antonin Scalia dissented from the majority opinion which struck down the Texas law banning sodomy. Scalia called invoking such foreign opinions a "dangerous precedent." He wrote:

The Court's discussion of these foreign views (ignoring, of course, the many countries that have retained criminal prohibitions on sodomy) is...meaningless dicta.[5]

In the 2002 *Atkins v. Virginia* death penalty case, Justice Stevens based his decision on the views of the "world community." In his dissent, Scalia said that it was...

...irrelevant what other countries think....the practices of the world community whose notions of justice are (thankfully) not always those of our people.[6]

Justice Breyer quoted eight words from the *Declaration of Independence* in attempting to justify use of foreign precedents in the case. Breyer said:

Willingness to consider foreign judicial views in comparable cases is not surprising in a nation that from its birth has given "a decent respect to the opinions of mankind."[7]

Justice Sandra Day O'Connor has been in the forefront of the justices who advocate basing Supreme Court decisions on foreign precedents. On a European visit in 1998, she predicted:

In the next century, we are going to want to draw upon judgments from other jurisdictions. We are going to be more inclined to look at the decisions of European courts and perhaps use them and cite them.[8]

In an October 2003 speech to the Southern Center for International Studies in Atlanta, Georgia, O'Connor said:

I suspect that over time we will rely increasingly, or take notice at least increasingly, on international and foreign courts in examining domestic issues.[9]

On October 28, 2004 O'Connor gave the keynote address at the dedication of the Georgetown University International Law Center Building. She said:

In a world that is increasingly interconnected, understanding international law is vitally important for today's legal scholars, lawyers and judges....International law often plays an important role in interpreting laws in the U.S. When gaps or inconsistencies exist, international precedents may be considered.[10]

The practice of sodomy was made a constitutional right on the final day of the 2003 Supreme Court session. The next day, five of the justices went to Europe. As part of their study of European law, three of the justices visited Jacques Chirac, the president of France. They discussed the death penalty—which, of course, is outlawed in France.[11]

Upon their return, Justice Ruth Bader Ginsburg joined Senator Hillary Clinton, former Clinton Attorney General Janet Reno and other liberal lawyers at a major "coming out party" of the American Constitution Society. The group which was formed in 2001 has received financing of $250,000 from leftist George Soros. The ACS goal was providing a liberal alternative to the conservative Federalist Society. The Federalists advocate nominating judges who believe in strict interpretation and application of the U.S. Constitution. In a widely publicized keynote, Ginsburg bragged:

Our island of lone ranger mentality is beginning to change...(Several justices) are becoming more open to comparative and international law.[12]

Justice Stephen Breyer has raised the question of whether with "globalization," our U.S. Constitution fits into the governing documents of other nations." When interviewed on ABC News by George Stephanopoulos, Breyer, in a rambling and somewhat disjointed statement, said...

...the world really, it's trite but it's true, is growing together...And how people are going to live together across the world will be a challenge and whether our Constitution and how it fits into the governing documents of other nations I think will be a challenge for the next generation.[13]

Phyllis Schlafly commented on Breyer's remarks, asking:

Where did he get the idea that the U.S. Constitution should "fit" into the laws of other nations? If a country can't make its own laws, how can it be a sovereign nation?[14]

Is Breyer's making our Constitution "fit into the governing documents of other nations" a step toward making the United States part of a one-world government? Does the U.S. Supreme Court have any Constitutional authority for making decisions based on foreign practices and customs so the United States can "fit in?"

The Court's openness to considering foreign influences is demonstrated by a series of events. They include:

In early 2004, the U.S. Supreme Court allowed the Commission of the European Communities to present a "Friend of the Court" oral argument in a case being considered.[15]

In the juvenile death penalty case, Roper v. Simmons, the Court accepted amicus briefs from 48 foreign countries and from the former Soviet dictator Mikhail Gorbachev. In February 2005 the U.S. Supreme Court heeded the pleas of Gorbachev and others and ruled that those who were seventeen years old when they committed murder could not be executed for their crime.[16]

The U.S. Supreme Court and its members have been reaching out regularly to foreign nations and their influence. Justices look to foreign influences on important issues like questions of morality, capital punishment and the death penalty. How long will it be before the death penalty, bans on same-sex marriage and other traditions and provisions of the Constitution go the way of longtime bans on sodomy and other perversions?

In other words, if the Supreme Court is allowed to continue looking to European and international precedents, traditional American freedoms and values could be in jeopardy. The trend towards consulting international agreements and laws of other nations is getting attention.

Jeffrey Rosen, in a *New Republic* article just before the 2004 presidential election, analyzed the possible effects of a Bush or Kerry election on the Court. He mentioned that opposition to court use of foreign precedents had become a rallying cry for social conservatives. But his article also quoted someone he termed a "more thoughtful conservative scholar," Jack Goldsmith of Harvard Law School. Rosen said Goldsmith has argued persuasively that...

...too much attention to international law could thwart U.S. constitutional traditions and reignite a domestic culture war.

There are, after all, dramatic legal and cultural differences between European and American views about free expression, privacy and due process. This means that, if judges become too willing to look to Europe, they may impose values on U.S. legislatures that the American public would be moved to resist.[17]

The resistance has already started. On March 11, 2004 the MSNBC web site featured a posting which said:

Stepping into the battle between the liberal and conservative judges on the U.S. Supreme Court, Republican House members are protesting the court's increasing use of foreign legal precedents in interpreting the Constitution.[18]

The article reported that Congressmen Tom Feeney of Florida and Bob Goodlatte of Virginia and 50 co-sponsors were proposing a non-binding resolution. It would express the sense of Congress that judicial decisions should not be based on foreign laws or court decisions. When interviewed Feeney said:

This resolution advises the courts that it is improper for them to substitute foreign law for American law or the American Constitution. To the extent that they deliberately ignore Congress' admonishment, they are no longer engaging in "good behavior" in the meaning of the Constitution and they may subject themselves to the ultimate remedy, which would be impeachment.[19]

The MSNBC article said, "The Feeney-Goodlatte resolution is in tune with Justices Antonin Scalia, Clarence Thomas and Chief Justice William Rehnquist. They hold that judges should look only to U.S. and British colonial precedents, such as Sir William Blackstone's *Commentaries on the Laws of England,* to interpret the U.S. Constitution."

The Feeney-Goodlatte approach could be a good start. The ultimate remedy, however, has to be selection of judges who will interpret and apply the U.S. Constitution according to what its words actually say. Impeachment of those who don't should be considered. It won't happen, however, until the American people are reeducated on the Constitution, its meaning and its importance.

CHAPTER XIII

WHAT CAN BE DONE TO RESTORE
GODLY, CONSTITUTIONAL JUSTICE?

*....the law is slacked, and judgment doth never go forth: for
the wicked doth compass about the righteous; therefore
wrong judgment proceedeth...O Lord, revive thy work in the
midst of the years..in wrath remember mercy.*
          —Habakkuk 1:4, 3:2

CAN AMERICA'S GODLY FOUNDATIONS be rebuilt today?
The influence of the media, the entertainment business, the schools
and universities, the government bureaucracy and many churches
has America deeply divided. Any realistic evaluation of the influence exerted by America's culture-shaping institutions indicates
that humanly speaking, there is no hope.

However, those who believe in an all-powerful, all-knowing,
all-loving Creator God are not limited to human solutions. God has
intervened down through history. When He has, He has worked
through people who have known Him and been yielded to Him. God
changes individual lives. He then uses those changed people to
change history.

General Douglas MacArthur pointed to the two possible paths the
nation can follow. Fifty years ago MacArthur said:

*History fails to record a single precedent in which nations subject
to moral decay have not passed into political and economic
decline. There has been either a spiritual awakening to overcome
the moral lapse, or a progressive deterioration leading to ultimate
national disaster.*[1]

The moral state of the nation has continued to deteriorate in the
years since MacArthur spelled out those alternatives.

From that standpoint, is there any reason to hope that God can
find people today willing to be used to reverse what has been done?
Can God find people who will prepare themselves so they can be
used to rebuild or replace America's character-shaping institutions?

The radicals of the 1960s now control the schools and universities, the media, the entertainment business, the government bureaucracy, and many churches. Until those institutions are recaptured or replaced, there can be no hope of returning America to its original Godly foundations.

Every citizen, the churches in which they are involved and the political parties of which they are part should be actively standing for traditional values. Abortion, sodomy, same sex marriages, and pornography are all evils God calls sin. They should be opposed by individuals and their groups and organizations. As important as such efforts are, none will succeed unless and until God chooses to intervene.

America needs a spiritual revival of the sort which transformed America in the twenty-five years before the War for Independence. The story of the Great Awakening which transformed America in the mid-1700s was recounted in the Introductory chapter. A few preachers like John Wesley and George Whitefield fueled the Great Awakening which transformed America. The nation was founded "under God."

God gave another such revival one hundred years later, but it was not primarily the work of preachers. Instead a few individuals prayed until God worked. God did work in the 1850s. Might God do it again? America doesn't deserve such a blessing—but God is a God of mercy and grace. How did such a nation transforming revival happen in the past?

In September 1857, Jeremiah Lanphier was a layman who worked on Wall Street in New York. He became concerned about the state of morals and the state of the churches in America. One commentator looking back said:

> It was a time of economic boom. Through stock market specula-
> tion many were becoming millionaires. Immorality, occult invol-
> vement and commercial and political corruption were rampant.
> Almost 2,000 immigrants were flooding into New York from
> overseas everyday. (Few had an understanding of the foundations
> on which America had grown great.) Spiritually, there was a
> growing rationalism including atheism and agnosticism. Man

would find and provide his own answers. Man was self-suffi-
cient.[2]

Much of that description could describe America today.

Lanphier and three associates decided to pray. They arranged to use the Dutch Reformed Church on Fulton Street in lower New York. They planned for an hour of prayer Wednesdays at noon. Handbills were distributed inviting...

...businessmen, mechanics, clerks, merchants and strangers to stop and call on God amid the perplexities incident to their respective associations.

Lanphier was alone when he opened the church at noon on September 23, 1857. As the hour unfolded several others showed. Varying accounts tell of a few more showing up for prayer during the next three Wednesdays.

Then on October 12, 1857, the stock market crashed. The money system collapsed in one hour. Banks failed, businesses closed, railroads went bankrupt.[3]

The next Wednesday the church was full. Daily prayer meetings were scheduled and before long 10,000 people were meeting daily across New York for prayer.[4]

The movement spread first to Philadelphia and Boston and then across the nation and to England. Millions of people came to Christ and went into the churches of America. Churches were transformed and brought back to their Bible roots. One commentator reported:

Businessmen began to pay off honest debts. Places of debauchery and taverns by the hundreds closed down. There was also an increased concern in helping the needy and destitute with great growth of volunteer work, and the financing of the work.[5]

The revival spread to the churches of slaves in the South. Then in the years which followed, the revival moved through the Confederate Army reaching as many as twenty-five percent of the soldiers.[6]

God appeared to be preparing people spiritually for the horror they would go through in the coming War between the States.

Even the *New York Times* noticed. On March 20, 1858, the Times reported:

The great wave of religious excitement which is now sweeping over this nation, is one of the most remarkable movements since the Reformation....It is most impressive to think that over this great land tens and fifties of thousands of men and women are putting to themselves in a simple, serious way, the greatest question that can ever come to the human mind—"What shall we do to be saved from sin?"[7]

All sorts of things happened. D. L. Moody, an 18-year old shoe clerk, was converted. As a layman, Moody became the greatest evangelist of the last half of the 19th Century. His work is still producing results today. In England, William and Evangeline Booth formed the Salvation Army.

Dozens of Bible schools were established. Lay people, preachers, and missionaries were trained. The great missionary effort which took the Gospel around the world came from what God did. Most of the familiar hymns of the faith being sung today were written by people who came to Christ in either the Great Awakening of the 1700s or in the years which followed the revival of 1857.

The political life of the nation, too, was turned upside down. The long powerful Whig Party struggled over slavery and other issues. Within three years, an upstart new party replaced the Whigs. In 1860, Republicans elected Abraham Lincoln and a Congress to support him.

In response to what initially was one man's burden to pray for his city and for America, America turned to God. However, nations don't turn to God; nations don't turn away from God. Only individuals can. When individuals truly come to the Lord, their cry should be like that of Saul of Tarsus, the persecutor of the First Century church. When he came face-to-face with Jesus Christ, he believed and cried out, "Lord, what wilt thou have me to do?" He became the Apostle Paul. The rest is history.

Much needs to be done. It can be done by individuals who from their hearts cry out, "Lord, what wilt thou have me to do?"

Good books on the problems produced by the courts have been written, published and distributed over the last fifty years. The authors look deeply into the societal tragedies produced by warped decisions of the Supreme Court. However, the books too often have focussed on "symptoms." Some propose actions to reverse Supreme Court decisions. Others put "band-aids" on symptoms. None have really faced the underlying problems. Even so, examining the books can be profitable. Two of the earliest were:

> John T. Flynn wrote <u>While You Slept: Our Tragedy in America and Who Made It</u> and <u>The Decline of the American Republic And How To Rebuild It</u>. The two books became runaway bestsellers in the 1950s.[8]

Flynn carefully exposed what he saw as a war to transform the United States from a constitutional republic into being part of an international socialist society. Flynn said those making the changes avoided the socialist "label."

Another pioneer visionary was Rosalie Gordon. Her book *Nine Men Against America*[9] was issued in 1958 and has been re-issued repeatedly. *Nine Men Against America* raised the alarm about the on-going decisions of the Supreme Court which were examined already in this book.

Flynn and Gordon proposed solutions. Tragically, however, their "solutions" only dealt with symptoms. None dealt with the real problems which caused the symptoms to develop. None of the remedies Flynn or Gordon proposed was adopted. Flynn came close to telling why. In the Foreword to *Decline of the American Republic* Flynn wrote:

> It is difficult to escape the feeling that most of the young men and women who passed through our colleges in the years from 1933 to the present time [1955] do not have the faintest conception of the type of government which Americans for a century and a half knew as the American Republic.[10]

Schools had deprived a generation of Americans of an understanding of the foundations of America's freedom and greatness. (They are the foundations spelled out in the first four chapters of this book.) Because the foundations had been ignored, most citizens didn't recognize how America was being changed. The remedies Flynn and Gordon proposed were never adopted. Schools were the problem in 1955 and remain the problem today.

If America is to be returned to her foundations, God-empowered people must recapture or replace the nation's schools. That won't happen until citizens first educate themselves on the foundational truths in the *Declaration of Independence*. Then they must educate their children and grandchildren. Some may do it through home schooling. Others seek a private or Christian school where the foundations are really understood and taught. Protecting our own families must be done first but that is not enough. Efforts must be made to return control of education to local communities so children of others can be trained also.

As the 21st Century opened, concerns continued to grow about what the Supreme Court is doing to America and its culture. Two excellent new books hit the best-seller lists. Mark Levin's excellent book, *Men In Black—How The Supreme Court Is Destroying America*[11] was released in early 2005. Phyllis Schlafly's *Supremacists—The Tyranny of Judges and How To Stop It*[12] was released a year earlier.

Levin proposes restoring the balance of power the founders intended between what were to be three co-equal branches of the federal government. To accomplish this goal, Levin envisions giving Congress the power to override Supreme Court decisions by a two-thirds vote of both Houses of Congress. Levin's proposal would limit the Court's almost total control over the States and the federal government's executive and legislative branches. A Constitutional amendment would be required to make the change.[13]

Efforts to adopt Levin's excellent proposal are not likely to succeed. His proposed change won't be any more successful than 40 years of efforts to ban abortion or return school prayer have been. Only God's intervention can make it happen.

In her *Supremacists* book, Phyllis Schlafly carefully documents...

> ...*how Courts have rewritten the Constitution, censored the acknowledgement of God, redefined marriage, undermined U.S. sovereignty, protected pornography, handicapped law enforcement, interfered with elections and reordered the culture and the way the States and their people live, work and govern themselves.*[14]

The book is an extremely valuable work. Schlafly examines many issues discussed earlier in this book in much greater detail.

Phyllis Schlafly goes far beyond what other authors and books have done in proposing solutions. If implemented, her well-thought out proposals could undo much of the damage the Courts have done for decades. Her specific proposals include:[15]

1. *The Senate rules must be changed to eliminate filibusters of presidential appointees so all are given the up or down advise and consent votes as the Constitution requires.*

2. *Article III, Section 2 of the Constitution should be used by the Congress to limit the jurisdiction of the Courts in matters such as marriage, acknowledgement of God, etc.*

3. *Congress should take action to prevent a single judge from using injunctions to block enforcement of referendums approved by voters in a state or locality. The ruling of just one judge can make it take years for an issue to wind its way through the federal court system before being finally resolved. [In May 2005, one federal judge in Nebraska overruled the vote of 477,571 Nebraska citizens. By a margin of 70% to 30% in 2000 voters adopted an amendment to the Nebraska constitution banning same sex marriages. Judge Battallion by his one vote overruled what 477,571 Nebraskans did. He declared that the State Constitutional Amendment they adopted by their votes was unconstitutional.]*[16]

4. *Congress should also prohibit State or federal courts from ordering any State or local entity to raise taxes. Constitutionally, raising taxes at the local, State and federal level is a legislative and not a judicial function.*

5. *The Courts should also be barred from continuing to use foreign precedents in interpreting and applying the U.S. Constitution. The issue was discussed in Chapter XII.*

6. *Congress should also stop the federal judges from awarding the outrageous attorney fees discussed in Chapter XI.*

7. *If Courts should refuse to abide by such remedies once they are enacted by Congress, impeachment should follow.*

Some corrective actions Schlafly proposes can be adopted by the vote of Congress. Others will require constitutional amendments. Almost all would produce filibusters in Congress and explosive demonstrations across America—unless and until God works again in a miraculous way as He has in the past. (Phyllis Schlafly's STOP

ERA has been the only truly successful effort which blocked a major thrust of the left in the last forty years.)

CONGRESS HAS RESPONSIBILITY AS WELL

The Courts and their betrayal of the vision and intent of the Founding Fathers get a lot of deserved attention. However, if members of Congress had taken their oath to uphold the Constitution seriously, Courts wouldn't have had the opportunity to approve unconstitutional actions of Congress and the Executive. One Congressman has been trying to force his colleagues in Congress to face the seriousness of their oath to uphold the Constitution.

Representative John Shadegg (R-AZ) has been trying for years to get Congress to face its responsibilities. Shadegg in each session of Congress for ten years has introduced *The Enumerated Powers Act.* The bill, if passed, would require that every newly introduced bill would include a statement setting forth the specific constitutional authority under which the law is being enacted. Requiring that all new laws would cite the specific constitutional provision which allows the Congress to legislate and the federal government to function in the proposed area would be revolutionary. It would force Congress to think about the Constitution.

Passage of the bill was blocked initially when House rules were rewritten to make Shadegg's proposal a rule of the House rather than a law. This could be a step in the right direction. However, a way has been found to evade the intent. On occasion, when a bill is introduced proposing a government action in the welfare area, for example, it is "justified" by citing the Preamble to the Constitution. The Preamble says:

We the People of the United States, in Order to form a more perfect Union, establish Justice, insure domestic Tranquility, provide for the common defense, promote the general Welfare, and secure the Blessings of Liberty to ourselves and our Posterity, do ordain and establish this Constitution for the United States of America. (Emphasis added).

While an attempt is made on occasion in Congress and elsewhere to give welfare programs Constitutional justification by citing the Preamble to the Constitution, the effort is not valid. The U.S. Supreme Court years ago ruled repeatedly that the Preamble doesn't actually authorize any government actions or authority. In *Jacobson v. Comm. of Massachusetts, 197 U.S. 11 (1905)* Justice Harlan's majority opinion set forth the clear reasons why the Preamble to the Constitution cannot be used as authority for governmental activity. Justice Harlan wrote:

> ...*Although that preamble indicates the general purposes for which the people ordained and established the Constitution, it has never been regarded as the source of any substantive power conferred on the government of the United States, or any of its departments. Such powers embrace only those expressly granted in the body of the Constitution, and such as may be implied from those so granted. Although, therefore, one of the declared objects of the Constitution was to secure the blessings of liberty to all under the sovereign jurisdiction and authority of the United States, no power can be exerted to that end by the United States, unless, apart from the preamble, it be found in some express delegation of power, or in some power to be properly implied therefrom.*

So, the Preamble cannot be used to justify Congressional actions and federal programs which are not specifically authorized in Article I, Section 8 of the body of Constitution. That section spells out the twenty or so areas in which the Congress can legislate and the federal government can operate.

Why is it important that Congressman John Shadegg's *Enumerated Powers Act* (H.R. 2458 in the 109th Congress) be passed? If a House rule places the same requirement on Congressmen introducing a bill which Shadegg's bill requires, what is the issue? If a House Rule is misused, it is a matter for the House to deal with. Because of the separation of powers, the issue cannot be taken to Court. If Shadegg's *Enumerated Powers Act* were to pass and be violated, a misuse of the *law* could be taken to Court.

Real remedies will face overwhelming odds from the media. But a God-empowered people can recapture the culture shaping institutions. God-empowered people, through prayer and evangelism, can see God reach and change the culture-shaping institutions—and the people in them.

Some good things are happening already. Talk radio and TV, the Internet and other forms of alternative journalism are punching holes in the "paper curtain." Media control has kept too many Americans in the dark for too long. Alternative news sources must be supported and encouraged.

Lack of teaching true history and sound principles of constitutional law creates another major obstacle.

RECAPTURE OR REPLACE LAW SCHOOLS

Shelby Sharpe, a prominent Texas attorney, has discussed how the courts have impacted the law and culture. Sharpe made a perceptive presentation at the *University of Alabama*[17] in 1986. He said the changes resulted from divorcing the legal system from its foundations in the law of God. Sharpe then said:

> *I don't care how many people you put on the Supreme Court of the United States or in the federal judiciary, until we change legal education, we're tinkering around up on the A-deck while the Titanic has got water coming in down below....and the ship is still going down...those of us in the legal profession have an obligation, a mandate, to take control again of legal education, and restore it to where it was...*[18]

Sharpe reported attending a conference of lawyers and theologians at the University of Notre Dame in 1981. Francis Schaefer (known for his *How Then Should We Live?* books and videos) spoke. Schaefer presented a challenge which Sharpe said, "...blew me apart." The challenge was:

> *If you Christian lawyers don't stand up for God in the courthouse, you tell me who will. It won't be the ACLU.*

Francis Schaefer then added these words:

> *Explain to me how you're going to answer that question to the Lord Jesus Christ on the day of judgment.*[19]

Sharpe said:

> *Years ago, the ungodly took over legal education. They didn't beat us, we gave it to them. God's people have to go back and reclaim what we gave up. That's our obligation, that's our challenge. Our founding fathers were willing to risk it all. What are we willing to risk?*[20]

Sharpe concluded his challenge saying:

> *We must return to the day where no human law is of any validity if contrary to God's Word. No lawyer should be permitted to step into any courtroom unless he is committed that he will take no position which violates Scripture. No judge should ever hand down a decision if it violates Scripture. That is where we came from. That is where we must be again.*[21]

For that to happen, the law schools must be recaptured or replaced as God works. Examining views expressed by influential law school professors shows how critical the need is.

The views of Alan Dershowitz at Harvard were shown in Chapter II. His book, *America Declares Independence*[22] trashes the *Declaration of Independence* and those who wrote it. His book shows that he has either done very poor research or that he has told deliberate lies about the religious commitment of Godly men among the founders. For example, Dershowitz described Benjamin Rush, a signer of the *Declaration of Independence,* as Thomas Jefferson's "close friend and fellow religious skeptic."[23] Dershowitz used a few random questions Rush raised while growing up to "prove" his position.

What are the facts? Rush, whom Dershowitz describes as a "religious skeptic," was a founder of The Bible Society of Philadelphia. He originated Sunday Schools in America.[24] Of religion in the schools, Rush in his *Essays* wrote:

> *...the only foundation for a useful education in a republic is to be laid in religion. Without it there can be no virtue, and without virtue there can be no liberty, and liberty is the object and life of all republican government....the religion I mean to recommend is that of the New Testament.*[25]

Any question about Rush's spiritual commitment was settled in his own autobiography. Rush gave this testimony of his faith in Jesus Christ, writing:

> *My only hope of salvation is in the infinite transcendent love of God manifested to the world by the death of His Son upon the Cross. Nothing but His blood will wash away my sins. I rely exclusively upon it. Come Lord Jesus—and take home Thy lost but redeemed Creature.*[26]

That should settle any question about Dershowitz being any sort of reliable witness—or teacher. Yet, as a prominent tenured professor at Harvard Law School, he is indoctrinating future lawyers and judges. Dershowitz is not alone. Susan Estrich is another. As a Professor of Law and Political Science at the University of Southern California Law School, she passes dangerous attitudes and viewpoints to her law students. They are the future judges and law makers. Here's an example:

> Estrich has been challenged in debates about contradictions in her public positions. Estrich strongly supported Anita Hill when Hill charged Supreme Court nominee Clarence Thomas with sexual harassment. However, Estrich opposed Paula Jones when Jones made sexual harassment allegations against President Clinton. Asked about the contradictions, Estrich replied, "You believe in principle. I believe in politics.[27]

Should Estrich be a model for future lawyers?

Estrich is not an isolated crackpot. She was a tenured professor at Harvard Law School before moving to USC Law School. She was the first female president of the Harvard Law Review. She was a special assistant to Stephen Breyer before he was named to the Supreme Court. Estrich also served as a law clerk to Supreme Court Justice John Paul Stevens. She was president of the Civil Liberties Union of Massachusetts, managed the Dukakis presidential campaign in 1988 and played a key role in President Clinton's campaigns. She appears frequently on FOX News to give the liberal Democrat point of view.[28]

The views of Estrich and those of Dershowitz permeate too many law school faculties. They are influencing and training future attorneys and judges. Law school teaching has produced judicial activism. That's why Matt Staver, who directs Liberty Counsel, a not-for-profit organization which defends life, the traditional family and religious freedom, says:

> ...the problem we face today with judicial activism begins in law school, where aspiring students are taught that law evolves and there is no objective truth.[29]

New law schools must be created or existing ones transformed. Rebuilding the teaching of law can be done by using a reversed version of the blueprint Roscoe Pound used in turning America's traditional Bible-based legal system upside down. Before Pound became dean of Harvard Law School he spelled out the law school changes needed to achieve sociological jurisprudence. Pound said law schools should equip future lawyers to work within the then traditional common law system of justice. While that was being done, Pound said, new generations of lawyers would be challenged and fitted to lead in the creation of true sociological jurisprudence.[30]

Using Pound's plan in reverse today would have new or reformed law schools...

> ...*teach the actual law by which courts administer and decide today, while challenging future generations of lawyers and judges to learn and return to the foundational documents and principles of the Biblically-based common law on which America grew great.*

CHURCHES MUST BE TRANSFORMED.

Most of America's mainline denominations have departed from the Bible. God's Word is no longer their absolute and final authority. Battles raged in the first half of the 20th Century in the mainline denominations and their colleges, seminaries, mission boards and publishing houses.

Questions were debated over the authority of the Bible. Did God create the world? Were Adam and Eve real people or just symbolic images? Did Noah's worldwide flood ever happen? Was Jesus Christ virgin born? Was He God? Did His death and resurrection atone fully for man's sins? Did man's nature and sin require salvation and the new birth? Early in the 20th Century, some Bible-believers separated and started new evangelical denominations. After about 1960, modernist Catholic teachers and theologians started down the path of questioning and unbelief which the liberals in the mainline Protestant churches walked earlier.

In the mid-1960s, some people in the Southern Baptist Convention, America's largest Protestant denomination, became concerned. Their seminaries were teaching future preachers doctrines which denied or were in conflict with the Bible. The accuracy and the authority of the Bible itself was being questioned.

Godly people became involved. They hoped to return the Southern Baptist Convention to its Biblical roots. Two dedicated young

couples met in New Orleans in March 1967. One was Paige Patterson, a student at the New Orleans Baptist seminary and his wife
Dorothy. The other was Paul Pressler, a successful Texas attorney,
and his wife Nancy. The Presslers were active Southern Baptist lay
people. Pressler later served as a judge in Texas Courts.[31]

Many people played important roles. Paul Pressler and Paige
Patterson provided leadership. Over a twenty year period, control
of the Southern Baptist Convention and its seminaries at the
national level were returned to Biblical foundations. The battle
continues in some local churches and SBC state associations. Much
can be learned from how victories were won. Pressler recalled that
up until then...

> ...conservatives had been able to win all the battles, but we kept
> losing the war [for control of the Convention] because we did not
> understand how the system operated.[32]

Divisions exist today in other churches, in the field of education,
in law, and in political organizations. Activists desiring changes in
an organization must learn how the system works—then use that
knowledge to make the change.

In 2002 Judge Pressler published his personal account of what
was done in the Southern Baptist Convention. It has been the only
successful effort made thus far to move an American mainline
denomination back towards its Biblical roots. Pressler's book, *A Hill
On Which To Die—One Southern Baptist's Journey,* [33] records the
strategies and the battles. It also gives a valuable insight into the
life, character and dedication of Paul Pressler. He spent years
standing for the authority of God's Word. His book can challenge
others to join the long battle to return America's churches to their
foundations.

Getting churches back to basic Bible doctrine is important but it
is not enough. There has been a real spiritual awakening in recent
years in America. However, the awakening has not been real
revival. Too much of the awakening has been man-centered rather
than God-centered. The emphasis has been on all that God will do
for those who come to Him for salvation. God does bless those who
come to Christ for forgiveness and a new life. Revival comes, however, when Christians begin to look, not for what they can get from

than God-centered. The emphasis has been on all that God will do for those who come to Him for salvation. God does bless those who come to Christ for forgiveness and a new life. Revival comes, however, when Christians begin to look, not for what they can get from God, but what they can do and be for God. That is the difference between a man-centered awakening—and a real God-centered revival. True revival changes people, a culture, a nation and its politics.

A true revival will affect the preaching from the pulpits. It did in the years during the Great Awakening before the War for Independence. A two-volume, 2,700-page collection titled, *Political Sermons of the American Founding Era, 1730-1805,*[34] shows that revived preachers of that era challenged their people with Bible answers to the problems facing the nation. They didn't limit themselves to doctrinal teaching. They made practical applications. They didn't concentrate on the feel good, how-to be successful sermons many hear today. If those preachers had, history may have been different. We could all be English citizens today.

Efforts are being made to have churches focus on what public schools are doing. Lay people within at least two denominations want churches to deal with the promotion of the homosexual lifestyle by public schools. In 2005, pastors and lay people within the Southern Baptist Convention and the Presbyterian Church in America (PCA) submitted resolutions to their national conventions. The resolutions proposed that parents should remove their children from public schools where immorality is tolerated and promoted. Among the leaders who cosponsored the Presbyterian resolution were Dr. D. James Kennedy of Coral Ridge Ministries and *World Magazine* publisher Joel Belz. Their resolution said that sending thousands of PCA children as "missionaries" to their unbelieving teachers and classmates has failed to contribute to increasing holiness in public schools. The PCA committee killed the proposal by a 35-10 vote.

The SBC committee also killed its proposal to remove children from public schools. SBC leaders Paul Pressler and Paige Patterson and Southern Seminary leader Dr. Al Mohler issued warnings about public school shortcomings. The Convention, however, after done. Laymen individually and pastors must provide stronger leadership.

What must be done can only be done when God's power is channeled through people yielded to Him. The night before the Lord Jesus went to the Cross, He told His disciples:

> *I am the vine, ye are the branches: He that abideth in me, and I in him, the same bringeth forth much fruit: for without me ye can do nothing.(Gospel of John 15:5)*

To be in Him and have His power and life flow through us, the individual must come to God first. An individual can only come to God one way. That way is through faith in Jesus Christ. The Lord Jesus said:

> *I am the way, the truth and the life. No man cometh unto the Father, but by me. (Gospel of John 14:6)*

Jesus has the right to make such an exclusive claim because He is God. He died for the sins of every person. He shed His blood on the Cross to pay the penalty for sin which is death. He was buried, but arose from the dead. The Risen Lord Jesus becomes the new life of those who believe and receive Him by faith into their hearts to be Savior and Lord.

Those who come to Him should cry out as the Apostle Paul did when he asked, "Lord, what wilt thou have me to do? (Acts 9:6)

An individual who is revived is ready to do God's bidding, no matter what the cost.

This chapter opened with a quote from the Old Testament book of Habakkuk. It spelled out situations then which were similar to those being faced today. Habakkuk said:

> *...the law is slacked, and judgment doth never go forth: for the wicked doth compass about the righteous; therefore wrong judgment proceedeth.*

Facing this situation, Habakkuk prayed:

> *O Lord, revive thy work in the midst of the years...in wrath remember mercy.*

That prayer should be the cry of every individual who has a true concern for America and its future.

CHAPTER XIV

TO RECLAIM THE CULTURAL INITIATIVE
CHANGE THE BASIS OF THE DEBATE

*...abortion [among other cultural ills and evils] is not the real
issue....Abortion is just a symptom. God is the issue! Abortion,
homosexuality, active euthanasia, and pornography are all just symptoms.
We have let others set the agenda for us. They have framed the debate and
we have been foolish enough to accept their terms of engagement. We must
reframe the entire rhetorical playing field in order to make God the issue
within the culture.*

—*Brad Bright, Author*
God Is The Issue

FOR OVER FORTY YEARS concerned and outraged people
have proposed Constitutional amendments to return prayer and
Bible reading to schools. Others have fought to reverse the *Roe v.
Wade* abortion decision. A Constitutional amendment banning
same-sex marriages is the issue as this book is being written.
Demonstrations have been staged, campaign speeches have been
given, petitions have been signed, people work and get more upset.
These are all good efforts. But they have been to no avail. Teachers
still can't allow students to pray in school, babies are being aborted,
and the courts have moved the controlling hand of the federal
government and its bureaucracy into every area of American life.
Why have there been so few results from so much effort?

Author Brad Bright in a valuable and insightful little book titled,
God Is The Issue,[1] tells why. Americans with traditional values,
despite a lot of effort and concern, have experienced on-going failure
to reverse the anti-God, anti-morality, big-government tide because
they have largely dealt with symptoms rather than the real cause
of moral decay. Brad Bright is the son of the late Dr. Bill Bright, the
founder and longtime head of Campus Crusade for Christ. In his
book, Brad Bright points to the reason for the on-going failures and
then proposes the real solution. Bright says:

Society has removed God from His place at the center of everything and given Him a seat on the sidelines. And we as the church have acquiesced to their agenda, and have joined the debate over symptomatic issues instead of clarifying that God is the logical and necessary starting point for all cultural debates.[2]

Bright explains that Bible-believing churches in America today...

...generally communicate with the culture in one of two ways. Either we preach the straight gospel without regard to the cultural and personal context, or we simply react defensively to the symptomatic cultural ills—such as homosexual behavior, abortion, racism, or pornography. Unlike Jesus, we have a difficult time using the cultural context as a relevant platform for making the God of the Bible the issue. Therefore, God comes across as largely irrelevant to the everyday life of the average American.[3]

Bright concludes:

In light of this, if the Bible is true, and the God of the Bible really exists, we must conclude that we have failed to effectively communicate "God" to our culture....We must begin focusing more of our efforts on curing the disease instead of just treating the cultural symptoms.[4]

That is vital, he says, because:

What we believe to be true about God will determine how we live and relate to those around us....When God becomes the central issue, debates about secondary matters [behavior] often take care of themselves and even go away.[5]

There is a clear cut scriptural basis for what Bright advocates as the way to recapture the cultural initiative. The Apostle Paul pointed to it in his epistle to the church at Colosse. In the first chapter, Paul recalled how he prayed continually that the Christians at Colosse would become all that they could be for God. It could happen, Paul said, as the Christians at Colosse grew in their knowledge of who the Lord Jesus Christ really was so that...

...in all things he might have the preeminence (Colossians 1:18-KJV).

The basis for the debates in which we engage or should be engaged must be changed. God must be made the issue in every debate. God must be at the center in every situation in our personal lives and in every issue in which we get involved. He must be given preeminence—first place in every discussion.

How does it work? Here is an example:

Several years ago, I (the author of this book) spoke at a political fund raiser and dinner in Milwaukee, Wisconsin. During the reception preceding the dinner I went to the bar to get some water. The woman bartender was so engrossed in a deep and heated debate with two very dedicated pro-life activists that she didn't notice me. When she saw me, she apologized and asked how she could help. I indicated that the wait was not a problem as I was fascinated by her arguments in support of a woman's right to choose an abortion when pregnant. She said, "Oh, really?" I said, "Yes, your position in support of a woman's right to choose is the best I've ever heard."

At this point the two pro-life activists (who I knew had been in jail for anti-abortion protests) were probably wondering who got this guy to speak for their conservative meeting. The woman was obviously pleased by my compliment and again asked, "Really? You were impressed by my arguments?" I said, "Yes, your logic supporting abortion is the best I've ever heard—*if there is no God.*"

The woman looked shocked and asked, "You mean God is concerned about abortion?" Her shock and her question points up the situation in much of American culture today. Almost all Americans believe in God. But they do not know Him and have no understanding or realization that He is concerned about everything in their lives and in our culture. To bring them to that realization is the only basis for recapturing the cultural initiative. It's the only basis for changing the debates and issues which divide Americans today.

Conservative Americans who oppose abortion, homosexuality, same sex marriage, pornography, gun control, and a lot of problems find themselves on the defensive. They are pictured or regarded as narrow-minded, uncaring individuals, who have no compassion. To win the battles Christians must move from defensive positions (which can never win) to offensive ones. They must learn how to switch the debate from the symptoms of abortion, school prayer, same sex marriage, racism, gun control to the cause of these sins. The God of the Bible must be made the issue.

To be effective requires that an individual knows the Bible and the issues. From that perspective, Christians are able in advance to think through how the basis of the debate can in kind, loving ways be switched from behavior (symptoms) to God and His position. That is the starting point.

Sometimes a question like the author of this book asked the woman bartender in Milwaukee accomplishes the switch. In other instances it can only be done by carefully thinking through how to switch the subject to God and His position before the "debate" even starts. Past experiences (and failures) can prompt development of new approaches before the next opportunity arises.

Many of the deep divisions in today's society stem from the fact that people think they or others have a "right" to engage in whatever behavior or action they want. Don't argue about the behavior or action. Simply ask, "Are you aware that the *Declaration of Independence,* our founding document, says that our rights come from God?" Most people will agree rather than appear ignorant. You then ask, "Do you believe that God would give you the right to...?" The individual may mumble "Yes." and try to support the desired "right." Switch the debate by saying that the Bible reveals everything about God and His actions. Say, "Can you show me in the Bible where God has given you the right to....?"

By such an approach, you have gone on offense and the other party is placed on the defensive. The other individual now either has to indicate that they don't know what the Bible says—or that they don't care what God says.

A wide variety of issues can be dealt with in this way. Consider gun control. Those who support controls on gun ownership aren't impressed by arguments based on the Second Amendment to the Constitution. Also, such debates probably won't be won by quoting all the statistics which show that crime hasn't increased in the thirty or forty states which recognize the right of an individual to own and carry weapons.

To overcome the emotions the issue provokes, the question to ask is, "Would you be interested in seeing what the Lord Jesus Christ had to say about guns and an individual's responsibility to protect himself and his family?" Immediately, the gun control advocate is placed on the defensive. They either have to agree and allow you to be in control of the on-going discussion—or indicate they don't care what God says. As was shown in the Chapter on the Biblical basis for the Bill of Rights and the Constitution, before the Lord Jesus went to the Cross in Luke 22:35-36 He said:

> *When I sent you without purse, and scrip, and shoes, lacked ye any thing? And they said, Nothing. Then he said unto them, But now, he that hath a purse, let him take it, and likewise his scrip: and he that hath no sword, let him sell his garment, and buy one.*

In that day, the sword was the means of self defense. If an individual didn't have a sword, Jesus said an individual should sell his overcoat if necessary to get one. The Lord Jesus, in this teaching, shows that people have a right of self-defense. Today, that is the right to keep and bear arms which is protected by the Second Amendment. In fact, the words of the Lord Jesus here appears to make having a means of self-defense not only a right—but a duty.

In this way, the basis for debate is moved away from what individuals think or feel about guns. God becomes the issue. Suddenly, who is in charge of the discussion?

The Same-Sex Marriage issue can be handled in the same way. The individual who simply opposes same-sex marriage comes through as uncaring and unfeeling. He or she is asked, "How can you deny two people who love one another the right to share their love and their lives together? Don't you know that denying them this right can stop them from visiting one another in a hospital, etc., etc., etc?"

A *switch-the-debate* question in such an instance can be, "How do you think God feels about two men or two women marrying each other?" Of course, most people think they know what God thinks about everything. Such a question is usually answered with statements like, "Well, I'm sure God wants people to enjoy life and help one another..." [Bright says, "Most Americans believe in the Bible because they do not know what it says."] Whatever the individual says that God must feel, we should smile and say, "Can you show me where in the Bible God says that?" Again, the supporter of same sex marriage is placed on the defensive.

Once the starting point of the cultural debate is switched from behavior to God, victory becomes possible. In his book, Brad Bright tells why, saying:

> ...*it is rationally impossible to begin with God (as defined by the Bible) and end with the conclusion that any immoral behavior is acceptable.*[6]

Bright then asks pointedly:

> *Why else has the other side worked so hard to remove "God" from the public square, beginning with public education?* [7]

The other side knows that when God becomes the issue, they lose.

Don't be obnoxious. Don't cram the Bible down the throats of the opponent. Lead them gently and lovingly to face the God of the Bible.

Will every one respond correctly? No. But even when they don't the effort may plant a seed of thought which will produce fruit. If this does not happen, the individual is made responsible for truth which will be faced on the Day of Judgment.

The Lord Jesus in John 12:47-48 spelled out the concept. He said:

> *And if any man hear my words, and believe not, I judge him not: for I came not to judge the world, but to save the world. He that rejecteth me, and receiveth not my words, hath one that judgeth him: the word that I have spoken, the same shall judge him at the last day.*

America's Biblical foundation, her *Declaration of Independence*, and her Constitution have been betrayed. Law schools, law practitioners, and many judges—from the lowest courts to those who sit on the bench of the Supreme Court—no longer uphold standards of morality and decency based on the Founding Fathers' intent and vision. Schools, the media, the entertainment business and the government and its bureaucracies have also deserted support for standards of morality and decency. America and her culture-shaping institutions must be returned to their foundations, and soon.

To help, get off the defensive. Go on offense. Learn how to reframe debates and discussions to make the God of the Bible the issue.

ACKNOWLEDGEMENTS

THERE ARE MANY LIVING AND DEAD to whom I owe much. On New Year's Eve in 1960, I read Notre Dame Law School Dean Clarence Manion's book, *The Key To Peace.* Manion opened my eyes to truth I never learned in my public school history and government classes—nor in classes at three universities. The United States is different from any other nation in history because our Founding Fathers discovered that men's rights come from God and that governments should be formed with the consent of the governed.

Barry Goldwater's challenge to devote myself to seeing that my children would have a more free nation than I had changed my life.

Phyllis Schlafly stayed in the battle for years when few wanted to listen. Her wisdom and work has encouraged me to keep going.

David Barton and Bill Federer collected the volumes of quotes of leaders who acknowledged that the United States was indeed founded as a nation under God. Their work has been invaluable.

Years before Roy Moore became Chief Justice of Alabama he pointed me to *Noah Webster's 1828 Dictionary.* The definition, "Religion is the duty owed to our Maker and the means by which it is fulfilled," helped me correctly understand the First Amendment.

Bob Baine, an attorney friend who has argued (and won) before the United States Supreme Court, helped me to understand the important difference between the common law and code law.

Katie Wollgast, a former student of mine who has learned a lot since I taught her, gave her time and effort to editing this book. Her challenge also helped me decide on the book's title.

Finally, I deeply appreciate my faithful wife, Elizabeth. As a recovering social worker, she learned before I did that government doesn't have all the answers. She has also persisted in helping me, a professional writer, learn to write so others will read.

I am also grateful for the people who over the years challenged me with the question, "If you died today, are you 100% sure that you'd go to heaven?" I hated them. But through their persistence and that of the Lord, I came to see and believe that Jesus Christ died not just for the sins of the world but for me personally.

Articles of Incorporation
of the
United States of America
known today as
THE DECLARATION OF INDEPENDENCE

WHEN in the Course of Human Events, it becomes necessary for one People to dissolve the Political Bands which have connected them to another, and to assume among the Powers of the Earth, the separate and equal Station to which the Laws of Nature and of Nature's God entitle them, a decent Respect to the Opinions of Mankind requires that they should declare the causes which impel them to the Separation.

WE hold these truths to be self-evident, that all men are created equal, <u>that they are endowed by their Creator with certain unalienable rights,</u> that among these are Life, Liberty and the pursuit of Happiness.—That to secure these rights, Governments are instituted among Men, deriving their just powers from the consent of the governed, that whenever any Form of Government becomes destructive of these Ends, it is the right of the People to alter or abolish it, and to institute new Government, laying its Foundation on such Principles, and organizing its Powers in such Form, as to them shall seem most likely to effect their safety and Happiness. Prudence, indeed, will dictate that Governments long established should not be changed for light and transient Causes; and accordingly all Experience hath shewn, that Mankind are more disposed to suffer, while Evils are sufferable, than to right themselves by abolishing the Forms to which they are accustomed. But when a long Train of Abuses and Usurpations, pursuing invariably the same Object, evinces a Design to reduce them under absolute

Despotism, it is their Right, it is their Duty, to throw off such Government, and to provide new Guards for their future Security. Such has been the patient Sufferance of these Colonies; and such is now the Necessity which constrains them to alter their former Systems of Government. The History of the present King of Great Britain is a History of repeated Injuries and Usurpations, all having in direct Object the Establishment of an absolute tyranny over these States. To prove this, let acts be submitted to a candid World. (Underline added)

He has refused his Assent to Laws, the most wholesome and necessary for the public Good.

He has forbidden his Governors to pass Laws of immediate and pressing Importance, unless suspended in their Operation till his Assent should be obtained; and when so suspended, he has utterly neglected to attend to them.

He has refused to pass other Laws for the Accommodation of large Districts of People, unless those People would relinquish the Right of Representation in the Legislature, a Right inestimable to them, and formidable to Tyrants only.

He has called together Legislative Bodies at Places unusual, uncomfortable, and distant from the Depository of their public Records, for the sole Purpose of fatiguing them into Compliance with his Measures.

He has dissolved Representative Houses repeatedly, for opposing with manly Firmness his Invasions on the Rights of the People. HE has refused for a long Time, after such Dissolutions, to cause others to be elected; whereby the Legislative Powers, incapable of Annihilation, have returned to the People at large for their exercise; the State remaining in the mean time exposed to all the Dangers of Invasion from without, and Convulsions within.

He has endeavoured to prevent the Population of these States; for that Purpose obstructing the Laws for Naturalization of Foreigners; for refusing to pass others to encourage their Migrations hither, and raising the Conditions of new Appropriations of Lands.

He has obstructed the Administration of Justice, by refusing his Assent to Laws for establishing Judiciary Powers.

He has made Judges dependent on his Will alone, for the Tenure of their Offices, and the Amount and Payment of their Salaries.

He has erected a Multitude of new Offices, and sent hither swarms of Officers to harass our People, and to eat out their Substance.

He has kept among us, in Times of Peace, Standing Armies, without the consent of our Legislatures.

He has affected to render the Military independent of and superior to the Civil Power.

He has combined with others to subject us to a jurisdiction foreign to our Constitution, and unacknowledged by our Laws; giving his Assent to their Acts of pretended legislation:

For quartering large Bodies of Armed Troops among us;

For protecting them, by a mock Trial, from Punishment for any Murders which they should commit on the inhabitants of these States:

For cutting off our Trade with all Parts of the World:

For imposing Taxes on us without our Consent:

For deriving us, in many Cases, of the Benefits of Trial by Jury:

For transporting us beyond Seas to be tried for pretended Offenses:

For abolishing the free System of English Laws in a neighbouring Province, establishing therein an arbitrary Government, and enlarging its Boundaries, so as to render it once and Example and fit Instrument for introducing the same absolute Rule into these Colonies:

For taking away our Charters, abolishing our most valuable Laws, and altering fundamentally the Forms of our Governments:

For suspending our own Legislatures, and declaring themselves invested with Power to legislate for us in all Cases whatsoever.

He has abdicated Government here, by declaring us out of his Protection and waging War against us.

He has plundered our Seas, ravaged our Coasts, burnt our Towns, and destroyed the Lives of our People.

He is, at this Time, transporting large Armies of foreign Mercenaries to compleat the Works of Death, Desolation, and Tyranny, already begun with circumstances of Cruelty and Perfidy, scarcely paralleled in the most barbarous of Ages, and totally unworthy the Head of a civilized Nation.

He has constrained our fellow Citizens taken Captive on the high Seas to bear Arms against their Country, to become the Executioners of their Friends and Brethren, or fall themselves by their Hands.

He has excited domestic Insurrections amongst us, and has endeavoured to bring on the Inhabitants of our Frontiers, the merciless Indian Savages, whose known Rule of Warfare, is undistinguished Destruction, of all Ages, Sexes and Conditions.

In every stage of these Oppressions we have Petitioned for Redress in the most humble Terms: Our repeated Petitions have been answered only by repeated Injury. A Prince, whose Character is thus marked by every act which may define a Tyrant, is unfit to be the ruler of a free People.

Nor have we been wanting in Attentions to our British Brethren. We have warned them from Time to Time of Attempts by their Legislature to extend an unwarrantable Jurisdiction over us. We have reminded them of the Circumstances of our Emigration and Settlement here. We have appealed to their native Justice and Magnanimity, and we have conjured them by the Ties of our common Kindred to disavow these Usurpations, which, would inevitably interrupt our Connections and Correspondence. They too have been deaf to the Voice of Justice and of Consanguinity. We must, therefore, acquiesce in the Necessity, which denounces our Separation, and hold them, as we hold the rest of Mankind, Enemies in War, in Peace, Friends.

We, therefore, the Representatives of the united States of America, in General Congress, Assembled, appealing to the Supreme Judge of the World for the Rectitude of our Intentions, do in the Name, and by the Authority of the good People of these Colonies, solemnly Publish and Declare, that these United Colonies are, and of Right ought to be, Free and Independent States; that they are absolved from all Allegiance to the British Crown, and that all political Connection between them and the State of Great- Britain, is and ought to be totally dissolved; and that as Free and Independent States, they have full Power to levy War, conclude Peace, contract Alliances, establish commerce, and do all other Acts and Things which Independent States may of right do. — And for the support of this Declaration, with a firm reliance on the Protection of divine Providence, we mutually pledge to each other our Lives, our Fortunes, and our sacred Honor.

Fifty-six men signed their names here, they did it for us.

Paul Harvey, in his book, *Our Lives, Our Fortunes and Our Sacred Honor*, told of the price paid by the fifty-six men who approved the Declaration on July 4, 1776. In the book, published by WORD Publishers, Harvey wrote:

> *Of the fifty-six, few were long to survive. Five were captured by the British and tortured before they died. Twelve had their homes...from Rhode Island to Charleston...sacked, looted, occupied by the enemy, or burned. Two lost their sons in the army. One had two sons captured. Nine of the fifty-six died in the war, from its hardships or from its more merciful bullets.*

They did indeed pledge "their lives, their fortunes and their sacred honor." Harvey's book detailed, name-by-name the price each paid to call for and win our independence and our right to freedom and self government.

REFERENCES

INTRODUCTION

1. Damelski and Tuchin, eds. The Autobiographical Notes of Cha rles Evans Hughes, (Harvard University Press, 1973) pg. 143. Quoted, John Whitehead, The Second American Revolution, pg. 21
2. Pound, Law and Morals, pg. 14
3. Letter, Thomas Jefferson, September 6, 1819, Jefferson Writings, Literary Classics of the United States, Inc., 1984, pg.1426, Quoted, Federer. America's God and Country Encyclopedia of Quotations, 1994
4. Thomas Jefferson on Politics & Government: Virginia.edu/jefferson/qu otations. Letter to Charles Hammond, 1821
5. Letter to Judge William Johnson, 1823, Thomas Jefferson on Politics & Government: Virginia.edu/jefferson/quotat ions
6. Video, Overruled, Coral Ridge Television Ministry, 2004
7. U.S. Supreme Court: Engel v. Vitale, 370 U.S. 421 (1962); Abington School Dist. v. Schempp, 374 U.S. 203 (1963)
8. U.S. Supreme Court: Roe v. Wade, 410 U.S. 113 (1973)
9. U.S. Supreme Court: Lawrence v. Texas, 539 U.S. 558 (2003)
10. Massachusetts Supreme Court: Goodrich vs. Dept. of Public Health (2003)
11. Third Circuit, Federal Appeals Court: Walz v. Egg Harbor Board of Education (2003)

12. U.S. Supreme Court: Stone v. Graham, 449 U.S. 39 (1980)
13. Madison, quoted by David Barton, The Myth of Separation (1991), pg. 120
14. Summary, Barton, The Myth of Separation (1991)
15. U.S. Supreme Court: A.B. Kirschbaum v. Walling (1942) 316 US 517 (1942)
16. U.S. Supreme Court: Wickard v. Filburn 317 US 111 (1942)
17. U.S. Supreme Court: Cert from 11th Circuit - No. 03-6821, Argued March 29, 2004-Decided May 24, 2004
18. Justice Anthony Kennedy, U.S. Supreme Court, Schiavo, Ex. Rel.; Schindler v. Schiavo, Michael et al, March 24, 2005; Associated Press, March 25, 2005
19. U.S. Supreme Court: Cert from 3rd Circuit - No. 03-218 Ashcroft v. ACLU, Argued March 2, 2004-Decided June 29, 2004
20. Washington Times, July 14, 2004
21. U.S. Supreme Court: McConnell v. Federal Election Commission, No. 02-1674 Argued September 8, 2003-Decided December 10, 2003
22. Wall Street Journal - Dec. 13, 2003
23. ADF, Sears, Foreign Jurisprudence Most Not Apply Here, August 5, 2003
24. ABC TV - This Week - July 7, 2003
25. Schlafly, The Supremacists, pg.48
26. Quote, The New American, August 9, 2004, pg. 44
27. Video, Overruled, Coral Ridge Television Broadcast, 2004
28. Bready, This Freedom Whence? Pg. xv
29. Nation Under God, Pg. 24
30. Ibid. Pg 25

31. Maxfield, Revival in America, Pg. 283
32. Ibid.
33. Quoted, Barton, The Myth of Separation, Pg. 249

CHAPTER I

1. Daily American, Poplar Bluff, MO, Sept. 4, 1996, pg. 7
2. Magruder, American Government, 1952 edition, pg. 73
3. Teachers' Manual, McGraw-Hill/Webster Division, Our Living Constitution, pg.75
4. A More Perfect Union, Houghton-Mifflin, 1991, Textbook Review, Michael Chapman, Eden Prairie, MN.
5. U.S. Supreme Court: Lawrence v. Texas, 539 U.S. 558 (2003)
6. Archived Column, WORLD on the Web, Cal Thomas, March 18, 2000
7. Ibid.
8. Scalia, Woodrow Wilson International Center for Scholars, Washington DC, March 14, 2005
9. The American Legion Magazine, October 2004
10. Ibid.
11. Damelski and Tuchin, eds. The Autobiographical Notes of Charles Evans Hughes, (Harvard University Press, 1973) pg. 143. Quoted, John Whitehead, The Second American Revolution, pg. 21
12. Letters, The American Legion Magazine, December 2004
13. Ibid.
14. Ibid.
15. Textbook Review, A More Perfect Union, Houghton-Mifflin, 1991, Michael Chapman, Eden Prairie, MN.
16. Thomas Jefferson on Politics & Government: Virginia.edu/jefferson/quotation s. Letter to Judge William Johnson, 1823
17. Quoted, None Dare Call It Education-1999, pg. 99

18. Quoted, Barton, The Myth of Separation, Wall Builder Press, 1991, pg. 176.
19. Times Argus, Barre, Vermont, January 31, 2004, pg. 1
20. Vermont Constitution 1793, Original and as updated
21. Associated Press, Bennington, Vermont Banner, January 31, 2004
23. Quist, FedEd, published by EdWatch, 1402 Concordia Ave., St. Paul MN 55104, pg. 16-19
22. CCE, We The People: The Citizen and the Constitution, pg. 192

CHAPTER II

1. John Quincy Adams, The Jubilee of the Constitution, 1839, pg. 54, Quoted by Barton, Original Intent, The Wall Builders, 1997, pg. 250
2. American Jurisprudence 2nd Edition, pgs. 552, 583-587
3. Legislative session debate reproduced in video, America's CENSORED Heritage, 2003, EdWatch, 1402 Concordia Ave., St. Paul MN 55104
4. Barnett, Restoring the Lost Constitution, Princeton University Press, 2004
5. Ibid., pg. ix
6. Ibid., pg. 1
7. McClellan, Liberty, Order and Justice—An Introduction to the Constitutional Principles of American Government, Third Edition, 2000, Liberty Fund, Inc., Indianapolis IN 46250.
8. Blackstone, Commentaries on the Law of England, Introduction, Section 2
9. Dershowitz, America Declares Independence, John Wiley & Sons, 2003
10. Claremont Institute, Review of Books, Summer 2004
11. John Quincy Adams, The Jubilee of the Constitution, 1839, pg. 54, Quoted by Barton, Original Intent, The Wall Builders, 1997, pg. 250
12. Jefferson, Notes on the State of Virginia, 1794, pg. 237, Quoted by Barton, Original Intent, The Wall Builders, 1997, pg. 334

CHAPTER III
References for this chapter, all of which are scripture citations are included in the text.

CHAPTER IV

1. U.S. Church of the Holy Trinity v. U.S. 143 U.S.457 (1892)
2. John Quincy Adams, The Jubilee of the Constitution, 1839, Quoted by Barton, Original Intent, The Wall Builders, 1997, pg. 224
3. Alexander Hamilton, Papers, Vol. 1, pg. 87. Hamilton was directly quoting from the Commentaries of Sir William Blackstone. Quoted by Barton, Original Intent, The Wall Builders, 1997, pg. 225
4. Encyclopedia Britannica, 2002 CD edition
5. Blackstone, Commentaries on the Law of England, Introduction, Section 2
6. Sir Edward Coke, .The Colombia Encyclopedia, Sixth Edition; MSN Encarta Encyclopedia Online 2005
7. John Jay, The Life of John Jay, William Jay, editor, 1833, Vol. II, pg. 385. Quoted by David Barton, Original Intent, The Wall Builders, 1997, pg. 225
8. James Wilson, Lectures on Law, College of Philadelphia, 1789-91: Andres, Works of Wilson (Chicago, 1896), Lecture 1, pg. 91-93; Reprinted, Eidsmoe, Christianity and the Constitution, Baker Book House, 6th printing, 1993, pgs. 44-45
9. John Eidsmoe, Christianity and the Constitution-The Faith of Our Founding Fathers, Baker Book House, 6th Printing, 1993, pg.83 Quoted by David Barton, The Myth of Separation,The Wall Builder Press, 1991, pgs. 92-93
10. The Papers of James Madison, University of Chicago Press, 1973, Vol. VIII, pg.293, widely quoted by David Barton, The Myth of Separation, pg. 178; Cousins, In God We Trust, The Religious Beliefs of the Founding Fathers, Harper, New York, 1958, pg. 256 and many others.
11. Washington, Farewell Address, September 19, 1796
12. John Adams,Message to Officers of First Brigade, Third Division of the Massachusetts Militia, Oct. 11, 1798, Works, Vol. IX, pg. 229, Referenced by David Barton, Original Intent, pg. 182
13. The Adams-Jefferson Letters, UNC Press 1959, Vol 2. pg. 412; Reprinted in Federer, America's God and Country Encyclopedia of Quotations, pg. 13
14. Patrick Henry of Virginia, Last Will and Testaament, Nov. 20, 1798; Plymouth Rock Foundation, Marlborough N.H., pg. iii; Reprinted in Federer, America's God and Country Encyclopedia of Quotations, pg. 289
15. Joseph Story, A Familiar Exposition on the Constitution, 1840, Reprinted 1986 by Regnery Gateway, Washington DC, pg. 314; Reprinted in Federer, America's God and Country Encyclopedia of Quotations, pg. 573
16. Joseph Story, Gary DeMar, America's Christian History, 1993, American Vision Publishers, pg. 113. Also Federer, pg. 574.

CHAPTER V

1. Georg Wilhelm Hegel, Columbia Encyclopedia, Sixth Edition 2001
2. http://www.philosophy pages.com/dy/
3. Richard Paul, 1990 - Center for Critical Thinking and Moral Critique, Sonoma State University, Rohnert Park CA
4. MSN Encarta Encyclopedia
5. Ibid.
6. Grolier Encyclopedia 2002
7. See Chapter 6

8. http://www.literature.org/ authors/darwin-charles/the-or igin-of-species
9. John Whitehead, The Second American Revolution, Crossway Books, 1982
10. Ibid.
11. Columbia Encyclopedia, Sixth Edition 2001
12. Blackstone, Commentaries on the Law of England, Introduction, Section 2
13. Columbia Encyclopedia, Sixth Edition 2001

CHAPTER VI

1. Pound, Law and Morals, pg. 14
2. Famous Alumni, Acacia Fraternity, http://www.acacia-unl.org/alumni/famous/poun d.php
3. Pound, ABA Speech, 1907
4. Whitehead, The Second American Revolution, Crossway Books, 1982
5. Pound, Five Lectures on the Philosophy of Masonry, Available on the INTERNET at http://www.masonicinfo.com /pikesphilosophy.htm
6. Review, De Rosa, The Ninth Amendment and the Politics of Creative Jurisprudence, Transaction Publishers, 1996, shttp://www.mises.org/mises review_detail.asp?control= 8&sortorder=issue
7. Available on the INTERNET at http://www.masonicinfo.com /pikesphilosophy.htm
8. Patrick Henry, http://www.southernmesseng er.org/historical_quotes.htm

CHAPTER VII

1. www.ali.org/Main.htm
2. American Legislative Exchange Council, 1129 20th Street N.W., Suite 500, Washington DC 20036, Phone: 202-466-3800. Cost: $10.00 plus S&H
3. Ibid.
4. Ibid., Obituary; Biographical Materials on Alfred Kinsey, The Kinsey Institute, www.in-

diana.edu/~kinsey/about/kin seybio.html
5. Kinsey, Sexual Behavior in the Human Male, 1948; Sexual Behavior in the Human Female, 1955 as analyzed and summarized in CRISIS Magazine, May 2004
6. Ibid.
7. Ibid., ALEC,pg. 1
8. Ibid.
9. Ibid., and Obituary cited above
10. Ibid.
11. Ibid.
12. Final Draft, ALI MPC (1962), pgs. 46-47, Appendix, The 1988 Modern Criminal Law, Cases, Comments and Questions, Second Edition, West Publishing Company, St. Paul MN.
13. James Jones, Kinsey, A Public/Private Life. 1997
14. Quoted, Ronald Ray, Study, The ACLU, et al v. A Foundations & Christian Morality, November 29, 2004
15. Dr. Linda Jeffrey and Colonel Ron Ray, RSVP America, (Restoring Social Virtue & Purity In America) NET: www..RSVPAmerica.org
16. Reisman, Kinsey: Crimes & Consequences, The Institute for Media Education, Crestwood KY, 1998, 2000 ShopNetDaily.com: $24.95; Kinsey, Sex and Fraud, Huntingdon House. Lafayette LA 1990.
17. Lancet, British Medical Journal, March 2, 1991, pg. 547
18. James Jones, Kinsey, A Public/Private Life. 1997 Quoted ALEC
19. A video copy of the BBC broadcast is available from RSVP America, P.O. Box 1136, Crestwood KY 40014.
20. Ibid., ALEC, pg. 3
21. Ibid., Crisis Magazine, May 2004, pg. 2
22. Hearings, Appendix and Report of the Special Committee to Investigate Tax-Exempt Foundations, Eighty-Third Congress (1955), Quoted Rene Wormser, Foundations: Their

Power and Influence, 1958, pg. 105
23. ALEC, pg. 9
24. Louis B. Schwartz, Book Review, Sexual Behavior in the Human Male, 96 University of Pennsylvania Law Review at 917, (1948), 24. Ibid. 25, Ibid.
25. Ibid.
26. Ibid.
27. Horack, 44 Illinois Law Review, at 156, 158 (1950) Quoted ALEC, pgs. 8-9
28. Pomeroy, Dr. Kinsey and the Institute for Sex Research, pgs.210-211 QUOTED ALEC pg. 8
29. California Assembly, Foreword to the Preliminary Report of the Subcommittee of the Assembly Interim Committee on Judicial System
30. ALEC, pg. 10
31. St. Louis Post-Dispatch, February 1, 2005
32. 52 Columbia Law Review, 1952, pg. 749 Quoted in ALEC, pg. 10
33. 65 Harvard Law Review-1952 Pg. 1128 Quoted ALEC pg. 11
34. ALEC pg.1
35. Dr. Meg Meeker, Epidemic: How Teen Sex Is Killing Our Kids, Regnery Publishing, 2002
36. Ibid. Quoted in ALEC, pg. 6
37. ALEC pg. 13

CHAPTER VIII

1. Annals of Congress 749, Quoted by Berger, Government By Judiciary, Second Edition, Liberty Fund 1997, pg. 155
2. Annals of Congress 439, Quoted by Berger, Government By Judiciary, Second Edition, Liberty Fund 1997, pg. 156
3. Barron v. Baltimore 32 U.S. (7 Pet.) 243 (1833)
4. Akhil R. Amar, The Bill of Rights and the 14th Amendment, 101 Yale Law Journal, 1193, 1246 (1902)

5. Forrest McDonald, Foreword, Government By Judiciary, pg. xvii
6. Berger, Government By Judiciary, Second Edition, Liberty Fund 1997, pg. 18
7. U.S. Supreme Court: Slaughter-House Cases, 83 U.S.(16 Wall.) 36 (1872), Quoted Berger, Government By Judiciary, Second Edition, Liberty Fund 1997, pg. 80
8. U.S. Supreme Court, Gitlow v. New York (1925)
9. Ibid.
10. Thomas Jefferson on Politics & Government: Virginia.edu/jefferson/quotations. Letter to Charles Hammond, 1821. ME 15:331
11. Ibid., Letter to William Johnson, 1823. ME 15:421
12. U.S. Supreme Court: Engel v. Vitale, 370 U.S. 421 (1962)
13. Abington School Dist. v. Schempp, 374 U.S. 203 (1963)
14. Seminar, Concordia Seminary,St. Louis, 5/26/98, Archived, freedomforum.org/templates/document.asp?documentID=9643
15. Ibid.
16. Thomas Jefferson on Politics & Government: Virginia.edu/jefferson/quotations. Letter to Samuel Miller, 1808. ME 11:428
17. Ibid., Letter to Rhode Island Assembly, 1801. ME 10:262
18. Ibid., Letter to William Johnson, 1823. ME 15:449
19. Ibid., ME 15:450
20. Ibid.
21. Ibid., Letter to Gideon Granger, 1800. ME 10:167
22. Ibid., Letter to Charles Hammond, 1821. ME 15:332
23. Lewis, A Man Born to Act, Not to Muse, New York Times Magazine, June 30, 1968, quoted by Berger, Government By Judiciary, pg. 156
24. Ibid., Lewis
25. Justice Potter Stewart dissent, Escobedo v. State of Illinois, 378 U.S. 478 (1964)
26. U.S. Supreme Court: Brewer v. Williams, 430 U.S. 387 (1977),

discussed in detail in Schlafly, The Supremacists, pgs. 77-78
27. U.S. Supreme Court: Minor v. Happersett, 88 U.S. (21 Wall.) 162 (1874, Quoted Berger, pg. 105
28. Berger, pg. 90
29. Ibid, pg. 132
30. Ibid., pgs. 5-6
31. Ibid., pg. 133
32. U.S. Supreme Court: Brown v. Board of Education, 347 U.S. 492-493
33. Berger, pg. 144
34. Pennsylvania v. Nelson 350 U.S. 497 (1956)
35. Cole v. Young 351 U.S. 536 (1956)
36. Slochower v. Board of Education of New York 350 U.S. 551 (1956)
37. Consul General for Yugoslavia v. Artokovic
38. News Record of 1957, Information Please Almanac, 1958, pg.11

CHAPTER IX

1. Sixth Circuit, Federal Court of Appeals, ACLU of Kentucky v. McCreary County, Kentucky (2003). For detailed discussion see www.restoringamerica.org/archive/education/banned_in_ky.html
2. Third Circuit, Federal Appeals Court: Walz v. Egg Harbor Board of Education (2003)
3. Ninth Circuit, Federal Appeals Court, Newdow v. Elk Grove Unified School District, 2002
4. U.S. Supreme Court: Everson v. Board of Education, 330 U.S. 1 1947
5. U.S. Supreme Court: Engel v. Vitale, 370 U.S. 421 (1962)
6. Limbaugh, Persecution, Regnery, 2003
7. Ibid., pgs. 19-20
8. Ibid.
9. Ibid., pg. 20
10. U.S. Supreme Court: Abington School District v. Schempp, 374 U.S. 203 (1963)
11. Ibid.
12. www.infidels.com/library/modern/corbett/abington.html

13. U.S. Supreme Court: Torcaso v. Watkins, 367 U.S. 488 (1961)
14. Ibid., 492-494
15. Story, Commentaries on the Constitution, 1833, Quoted Federer, America's God and Country Encyclopedia of Quotations, pg. 572
16. Ibid., pg. 574
17. U.S. Supreme Court: Stone v. Graham, 449 U.S. 39 (1980)
18. Ibid.
19. Ibid.
20. Ibid.
21. Madison, quoted by David Barton, The Myth of Separation (1991), pg. 120
22. U.S. Supreme Court: Church of the Holy Trinity v. U.S., 143 U.S. 457 (1892)
23. U.S. Supreme Court: Lee v. Weisman, 505 U.S. 577 (1992)
24. U.S. Supreme Court: Santa Fe Independent School District v. Doe, 530 U.S. 290 (2000)
25. Sixth Circuit, Federal Court of Appeals, ACLU of Kentucky v. McCreary County, Kentucky (2003). For detailed discussion see www.restoringamerica.org/archive/education/banned_in_ky.html
26. Souter, Supreme Court, McCreary County, Kentucky, et al. v. American Civil Liberties Union of Kentucky et al.
27. Ibid.
28. Opinion, Judge Myron Thompson, Federal District Court, Middle District of Alabama, Glassroth v. Chief Justice Roy Moore, November 18, 2002, pg. 2
29. Ibid., pg. 35
30. Ibid., pg. 7
31. Ibid., pg. 63
32. Ibid., pgs. 59-61
33. Trial of Chief Justice Roy Moore, State of Alabama Court of the Judiciary, Part 2, pgs. 9-10
34. Ibid., pg. 9
35. Ibid.
36. Ibid.
37. Ibid.
38. Ibid., pgs. 50-51

39. Roy Moore, Revival Fires Campmeeting, Branson MO, April 1, 2004

CHAPTER X

1. United States District Court for the Western District of Missouri, Southern Division, Carrie M. Roat, Plaintiff vs. Gregory E. Thompson, Superintendent of the Humansville R-IV School District, and the Humansville R-IV School Board and two other listed school officials; Second Amended Complaint, May 21, 2004
2. Ibid., Counts 10-12
3. Ibid., Count 15
4. Ibid., Count 17
5. Ibid., Count 19
6. Ibid., Counts 33-38
7. St. Louis Post-Dispatch, July 30, 2004, Pg. B7
8. Memorandum, Dee Wampler, RE: Roat v. Gregory Thompson-et all, August 17, 2004
9. See Chapter 11, ACLU Finds Pot of Gold at the Foot of the Cross
10. Letter, Thomas A. Mickes, Doster Mickes James & Ullom LLC, August 17, 2004
11. Ibid.
12. Ibid.
13. Thompson, Six Page Statement to the Humansville R-IV School Board
14. Ibid.
15. Ibid.
16. Ibid.
17. Ibid., Board Choice 1
18. Ibid., Board Choice 2
19. Ibid., Board Choice 3
20. Agreement of Separation, Severance and Release, Humansville School Board, August 24, 2004
21. Letter of Recommendation, Humansville School Board, August 24, 2004
22. Ibid.

CHAPTER XI

1. American Legion Magazine, February 25, pg. 20

2. Ibid.
3. Ibid.
4. See Chapter 9
5. American Legion, pg. 20
6. Ibid. pgs. 20-22
7. Human Events, June 22, 2004. Net www.humaneventsonline/article.php?id=4259
8. American Legion Magazine, pg. 22-24
9. Baptist Press, March 11, 2005
10. Ibid.
11. Ibid.
12. Ibid.
13. Ibid., American Legion Magazine
14. American Legion Magazine, May 2005, pg. 32
15. Nat Hentoff, Village Voice, January 18, 2005. See at www.campus-watch.org/pf.php?id=1527
16. Whistleblower Magazine, Worldnetdaily.com, December 2004, pg. 4
17. William Donahue, The Twilight of Liberty and The Legacy of the ACLU
18. Baldwin, Letters From Soviet Prisons quoted by William Donahue, The Twilight of Liberty and The Legacy of the ACLU
19. Baldwin, Liberty Under The Soviets quoted by William Donahue, The Twilight of Liberty and The Legacy of the ACLU
20. Ginsberg Bio, FindLaw Constitutional Law Center: Supreme Court: Justices: Ruth Bader Ginsberg NET: http://supreme.lp.findlaw.com/supreme_court/justices/ginsberg.html
21. http://www.nhclu.org/publications/100_greatest.htm
22. American Legion Magazine, February 2005, pg. 22
23. The Phyllis Schlafly Report, Vol. 37, No. 2, September 2003
24. American Legion Magazine, February 2005, pg. 20-22
25. Human Events, June 22, 2004.
26. Schlafly, The Supremacists: The Tyranny of Judges and How to Stop It-Spence Publishing Co.

CHAPTER XII

1. Justice Stephen Breyer, U.S. Supreme Court: Knight v. Florida, 528 U.S. 990 (1999), quoted by Phyllis Schlafly, Washington Times, August 13, 2003
2. Justice John Paul Stevens, U.S. Supreme Court: Atkins v. Virginia, 536 U.S. 304 (2002)
3. Ibid., Justice Clarence Thomas, Dissent
4. Justice Anthony Kennedy, U.S. Supreme Court: Lawrence v. Texas, 539 U.S. 558 (2003)
5. Ibid., Justice Antonin Scalia, Dissent
6. Justice Antonin Scalia, Dissent, Atkins v. Virginia, 536 U.S. 304 (2002)
7. Tom Curry, MSNBC News, March 11, 2004, http://msnbc.msn.com/id/4506232/
8. Justice Sandra Day O'Connor, Quoted: http://www.neusysinc.com/columnarchive/colm0198.html
9. Tom Curry, MSNBC News, March 11, 2004, http://msnbc.msn.com/id/4506232/ Column, Phyllis Schlafly, April 14, 2004, online at http://eagleforum.org/column/2004/apr04/04-04-14.html
10. Justice Sandra Day O'Connor, University News, Georgetown University, http://www1.georgetown,edu/explore/news/?ID=1363
11. Associated Press, Washington Post, August 2, 2003; The Hill, July 15, 2003
12. Ibid.
13. Phyllis Schlafly, Washington Times, August 13, 2003, and http://www.neusysinc.com/columnarchive/colm0198.html
14. Ibid.
15. Column, Phyllis Schlafly, November 10, 2004
16. Ibid.
17. Jeffrey Rosen, New Republic, quoting Jack Goldsmith, Harvard Law School; http://www.ocnus.net/cgi-

9. Gordon, Nine Men Against America, Devin-Adair, 1958; Reissued Western Islands, Appleton WI, 1961, 1965,

10. Flynn, pg. ix

11. Levin, Men In Black—How The Supreme Court Is Destroying America, Regnery, 2005

12. Schlafly, Supremacists—The Tyranny of Judges and How To Stop It, Spencer, 2004

13. Levin, pgs. 197-202

14. Schlafly, pg. v.

15. Ibid., pgs. 113-149

16. The Alliance Alert, Alliance Defense Fund, May 16, 2005: http://www.alliancealert.org/index.php?ID=441

17. Sharpe Video, Understanding the Times, Summit Ministry, Manitou Springs CO 80829.

18. Ibid.

19. Ibid.

20. Ibid.

21. Ibid.

22. Dershowitz, America Declares Independence, John Wiley & Sons, 2003

23. Ibid., pg. 79

24. Barton, Benjamin Rush, Signer of the Declaration, WallBuilder Press, 1999, pg. 100

25. Rush, Essays, On the Mode of Education Proper in a Republic, pgs. 57-73, Quoted by Barton, Benjamin Rush, Signer of the Decla ration, WallBuilder Press, 1999, pgs. 45-46

26. Rush, Autobiography, 1800, Quoted by Barton, pg. 32

27. The Schwarz Report, Vol. 45 #2, February 2005; Debate, Did Clinton Harass Paul Jones?, Nov, 27, 1996 http://slate.msn.com/id/3628/; Q u o t e d http://www.renewamerica.us/columns/campbell/031128

28. USC Faculty of Law Biography,

29. Staver, An Antidote to "Judges Gone Wild", May 5, 2005, Liberty Counsel, liberty@lc.org

30. Chapter VI

31. Pressler, A Hill on Which To Die, Broadman & Holman Publish ers, Nashville, 2002, pgs 57-60

32. Ibid.

33. Ibid.

34. Liberty Fund, Inc., 8335 Allison Pointe Trail, Ste 300, Indianapolis IN 46250.

CHAPTER XIV

1. Bright, God is the Issue, 2003, New Life Publications, 375 Highway 74 South, Suite A, Peachtree City GA 30269

2. Ibid., pg. 16

3. Ibid.

4. Ibid., pgs. 16, 23

5. Ibid., pgs, 17, 53

6. Ibid., pg. 28

7. Ibid.

INDEX

INDEX

SCRIPTURE REFERENCES

SUPREME COURT DECISIONS